Toyota

Toyota

K. Dennis Chambers

Corporations That Changed the World

GREENWOOD PRESS
Westport, Connecticut • London

This book is dedicated to my honored Uncle Chuck, known to many as Charles G. Coleman, Captain (Retired), United States Navy

Library of Congress Cataloging-in-Publication Data

Chambers, K. Dennis, 1943–
  Toyota / K. Dennis Chambers.
    p. cm. — (Corporations that changed the world, ISSN 1939–2486)
  Includes bibliographical references and index.
  ISBN 978–0–313–35032–0 (alk. paper)
 1. Toyota Jidosha Kabushiki Kaisha—History.   2. Toyota Jidosha Kabushiki
Kaisha. I. Title.
  HD9710.J34T621723   2008
  338.7′62920952—dc22   2008012988

British Library Cataloguing in Publication Data is available.

Library of Congress Catalog Card Number: 2008012988
ISBN: 978–0–313–35032–0
ISSN: 1939–2486

First published in 2008

Greenwood Press, 88 Post Road West, Westport, CT 06881
An imprint of Greenwood Publishing Group, Inc.
www.greenwood.com

Printed in the United States of America

The paper used in this book complies with the
Permanent Paper Standard issued by the National
Information Standards Organization (Z39.48–1984).

10 9 8 7 6 5 4 3 2 1

Contents

Introduction

The first miracle of the Toyota Motor Corporation is that it exists at all.

Every generation of the founding Toyoda family (this slight name change is explained in a later chapter) has had to endure a crisis, from regional wars to world wars, from internal civil conflict to outside invaders, from local economic downturns to global depressions. Few international manufacturers have had to pick themselves up from the nearly complete devastation of atomic explosions and start over in a modern economy with no infrastructure and little hope for the future. Few carmakers have had to fight their own country's red tape for the right simply to make and sell automobiles. And no other carmaker has started its business life as a producer of small industrial looms for weavers and textile companies.

The second miracle of the Toyota Motor Corporation is that it has singlehandedly—and in the face of massive international scorn—created the philosophies and techniques that are now commonplace in nearly every manufacturing facility in the world. Whether you are a football-manufacturing plant in Peru or a maker of airplane engines in Sweden, chances are you are using Toyota-style management and manufacturing techniques to keep your enterprise profitable.

The third miracle of Toyota is that it is, right now, engineering the future of automobiles and their drivers. When it comes to delivering a car that combines eye-popping gas mileage (pushing toward 60 miles per gallon in normal driving) with freeway-worthy power, there's Toyota and then there's everyone else. No one was surprised when Toyota, in 1997, became the first carmaker to produce a powerful, high-quality "hybrid" car that used a combination of electricity and fossil fuel for power. Nor was anyone surprised when Toyota's famous Prius (pronounced PREE-us) hybrid won a shelf-full of awards, including Car of the Year in Japan (1998), North American Car of the Year (2004), and European Car of the Year (2005).

Tellingly, no one who works for Toyota would see any of these achievements as "miracles." Unless they, like some cynics these days, see hard work as miraculous.

We live in the Age of Excellence. Pick up any business magazine, listen to any CEO on a radio or television interview, check out any business-related Web site, and chances are you'll run across a description of the company in question that includes "excellence." We are committed to excellence, the ads say. We are driven to provide you an excellent experience, the Web site declares. Our customer service is excellent. Our products and our guarantees are excellent.

There's only one problem with all of this. In most cases, it isn't true.

Any unusually successful accomplishment requires unusual focus on the task. "Champions pay the price" is an old saying, but one that is true. A champion such as the baseball great Ted Williams, for example, spent most of his waking hours learning and practicing how to hit a baseball coming straight at him at 96 miles per hour. Tiger Woods has a practice regimen that keeps him at the top of the list of the greatest golfers of the twenty-first century. Dorothy Hamill, Olympic ice-skating champion in 1976, was legendary for her practice routines that allowed her to stop only when the move she was practicing was executed perfectly. The list of people who have achieved significant things by working many times harder than most is not long.

Toyota is in that list.

Such a total focus is a requirement for any individual or organization that desires to achieve excellence in any endeavor. In business, many companies claim to have that focus. But few actually practice it.

Consider why. Managers come and go in any company. They may emphasize this or that, but seldom with a consistency that spans generations. Corporations write procedural manuals but seldom use them as operating bibles on the factory floor. Most companies in industrialized nations look ahead one or two quarters at best. And most American corporations frown on—even punish—people who reveal problems with the production line or with quality or with service.

Not so Toyota. People who find and fix problems are rewarded in a Toyota plant. Toyota created a whole philosophy, called *kaizen* (ky-zen), that teaches workers the value of continuous incremental improvement every day. Toyota nurtures its employees and keeps trying to put people in positions where they fit best. Managers use operating manuals the way Supreme Court Justices use the U.S. Constitution—studying it word for word, practice for practice. And Toyota has plans that extend 20 years out into the future. They are in business for the long haul and take pains every day to remind people of that fact. When a manufacturer focuses time and effort and money on making every small thing excellent, it will be excellent in the big things.

The cost for doing all of this every day is breathtakingly high. For world-class athletes, the cost is working until darkness falls, or until hands bleed, or until muscles fail under the strain. The same is true for companies. Almost alone among all the world's product makers, Toyota pays that price.

The sheer force of will that enabled Toyota's founders and subsequent leaders to guide the corporation through economic peaks and valleys, through war and peace, through family squabbles and decades of prejudice against anything "made in Japan" is only half of the story. The second half is the ancient and intricate Japanese culture itself, an island culture that has tried mightily to maintain the purity of bloodlines and to prevent the leavening of its religions and history by outside invaders. Sometimes those invaders arrived with gunships blazing and bombs dropping; other times they arrived to proselytize in favor of non-Japanese religion or European business practices that emphasized profit over even honor and family. Through all these centuries of upheaval and destruction, the Japanese people held fast to their core identity, prevailed, and then flourished.

The story of the Toyota Motor Corporation is mainly the story of an extraordinary group of entrepreneurs and engineers who performed miracles every day. And it is also, in part, a brief look at the great island nation of Japan in the modern world.

Chapter One

Origins and History

The story of the Toyota car-making family begins in Japan at the turn of the twentieth century. However, like any great story, its beginnings are not so clear and go much farther back in time. The people who show up on history's stage are themselves the products of the culture that bred them. Toyota, more than anything else, is a Japanese company. To understand the company, we must understand a little of Japan.

GEOGRAPHY IS DESTINY

While many people think Japan is one island, it is actually more than 3,000 islands, most of which have mountains and volcanoes. The islands themselves are essentially hard volcanic rock with a thin layer of topsoil and few natural mineral resources, although there is some gold and silver. Only about one-fifth of the land is suitable for agriculture or the growth of cities; the rest consists of tree-covered mountains. Mount Fuji, the cone-shaped and snow-covered international symbol of Japan, is a dormant volcano that was last heard from in 1708. The four largest of Japan's islands, Honshu, Kyushu, Hokkaido, and Shikoku, make up about 97 percent of the nation's land, which in total (145,833 square miles) is slightly smaller than California. The land mass of the United States, by contrast, is more than 3.7 million square miles.

Most Japanese live within an hour's drive of the sea; the nation is considered to have more coastline than land mass. For centuries, its primary industry has been fishing. The beautiful Inland Sea, in the southwest corner, teems with marine life, and the world's oceans lie at the island's doors. The country's crops include barley, oats, and wheat; apples and citrus fruits; tea; and, of course, rice.

Since usable land is so scarce and so valuable, almost from the beginning there has been tension between agriculture and industry. Both fight for the same acreage. For most of Japan's history, that acreage was reserved for rice.

Even with poor soil, Japanese rice farmers have been immensely productive. From prehistoric times, at least in the southern half of the country, they have been able to count on only one rice crop in a season. Rice, the main source of nutrition for all human beings in the country, was easier to grow in countries to the south, such as Vietnam and the Philippine Islands, where peasants routinely brought in three crops a year. In Japan, the people had to be industrious and imaginative, or they would starve. So they cut into the sides of hills and mountains. They built dams and drainage pools on the upper slopes where sunlight could find the seeds. And they watched the crop tenderly and anxiously until it was safely harvested. To break the cycle, to try farming in a new way, to abandon the old ways that were certain to work, or even to leave the farm for a potentially better life in town was to invite starvation for the clan.

Since the country is resource-poor, it must import nearly everything it needs for growth and productivity. For example, Japan has virtually no domestic oil supplies—a fact that led directly to the Empire's decision, under threat of embargo from the Allies, to bomb Pearl Harbor at the beginning of World War II. Geography often dictates history.

Japan's biggest resource is its 127 million people, who are highly educated and fiercely independent. (America, with just over twice the population of Japan, has 30 times the land mass and thousands of times the natural resources.)

The existence of this isolated, multi-island nation first became known to the world in early Chinese writings nearly 2,000 years ago. The writings suggested an exotic and secretive people who desired nothing more than to be left alone.

Comparisons between Japan and the United States

Japan	*United States*
Limited land	Unlimited land
Minimal natural resources	Nearly unlimited natural resources
Ancient culture	The New World
Emphasis on family	Emphasis on the individual
Traditional	Nontraditional
Strict government controls	Few government controls
Cooperation	Competition
Slow to industrialize	Quick to industrialize
Frugal	Free-spending
Indirect	Direct
Isolated from the world until 1853	Open from the beginning
Harmony	Conflict
Polite	Assertive

SAMURAI SPIRIT

As so many preindustrial societies do, the people organized themselves into clans or tribes, gradually giving power to a centralized authority that became known as the Shogunate. Even so, the clans solidified into a traditional patriarchal culture with clear lines of respect tending upward. One's social betters were to be bowed to and given tribute in the form of goods and money. The clans arranged for their own armed forces, which in themselves developed clear lines of authority. If one did not clear the road so that a superior might pass, or failed to bow to a superior, or otherwise gave offense even inadvertently, the punishment was often severe and long-lasting. The warrior professionals became known as samurai. Their weapon was the short or long sword, at which they were astonishingly proficient. And if, while serving their lord, they were to take too many chickens from a village, or slice too deeply an unfortunate peasant who displeased them, well, there was none to protest their behavior. The people served the local magistrates, who served the regional rulers, who served the Shogunate, who ruled in the name of the divine emperor.

Thus organized into stratified societies, with power going to political and military leaders, the peasants worked the rice paddies generation after generation, the warriors served their militia lords and kept the civil peace, and all of the people seemed to agree that this was an arrangement upon which the gods smiled.

Sometime around 1540, a Chinese merchant ship anchored near Kyushu, one of the southern islands, looking to trade. On board were several Portuguese adventurers who were the first known Westerners to set foot on its shores. They discovered that the Japanese were indeed an aggressively insular people who wanted nothing to do with Western culture or religion. The Portuguese seafarers had brought with them a Western invention that was new to the Japanese: a sticklike weapon that ignited and fired a projectile fast and far. The Japanese quickly took to the new weapons, called guns, and used them for a generation in battle, along with the swords of the samurai.

But the gun was not the right kind of weapon for the culture. It killed or wounded indiscriminately, from afar, and carried with it no honor. Anybody could shoot a gun—a child, a coward, a dishonorable person. Unlike a sword, a gun required little skill to be lethal. Around 1616, the nation had had enough of these Western weapons and declared guns to be inappropriate, along with Western religion and its attendant missionaries.

The demand for guns inside Japan essentially disappeared, while the market for swords rose. Japan and its warriors were swordfighters, not gunfighters. In the skills of using the sword there was honor. In modern Japan, private gun ownership is illegal.

Japan looked to their west and saw the chaos in China's culture that the opium trade and other dealings with Westerners had wrought. The nation put up philosophic barriers to all outside culture.

The word spread, and the rest of the world left Japan alone until a warm July day in 1853, when yet another Western culture came knocking. And these visitors carried guns. Big guns.

COMMODORE PERRY SENDS GREETINGS

On that day, Commodore Matthew Perry and four "black ships" of the United States Navy sailed into Tokyo Bay. The ships were black because they were heavy, seaworthy vessels bristling with cannons and covered in tarry pitch to prevent leaks during the long voyage. Their appearance as obvious warships stunned the local citizens and politicians. The people of Japan at this time had a long tradition of wars and insurrections and samurai warriors. But they had never seen anything like the four black ships and their booming guns. They stared in growing horror at the evidence before their own eyes that there was no resisting such a nation with such force behind it.

Commodore Perry delivered a letter from U.S. President Millard Fillmore to the Emperor of Japan, inviting trade. It was an invitation delivered with an iron fist. The Americans were battling the British for dominance in the lucrative China trade, involving delicate silks, exotic woods, and fragrant spices. They needed a coal-producing port where they could refuel their merchant steamships and so save precious cargo space for the silks and spices and teas of China. In addition, the American whaling industry, although the market for whale oil was diminishing, still found itself in need of great quantities of coal in order to boil whale fat and render the great creatures into products directly after harpooning them. And so Commodore Perry was asking politely, but with loaded cannons behind him.

The Americans were not the first raiders to drop anchor in Japanese waters.

From time immemorial, Japan has seen itself as a divine nation. Its people saw themselves not only as different in nature from the Chinese, Siamese, Cambodians, and others in their Pacific Rim but also as superior to all of them. The people labored hard to grow their rice. They gathered themselves into villages and family clans and passed on the strict traditions that had worked so well for so many centuries. These traditions all were built on the facts of limited arable land, limited resources, and limited space for population growth. The peasants labored in the same way for centuries, living and working closely together and passing on these traditions, while the political and military leaders appeared and disappeared like the seasons. For most Japanese, nothing changed year after year, generation after generation. The people worked the land and the rice paddies, raised their children, cared for and buried their elders, and lived their lives in a predictable sameness.

Such isolation and self-satisfaction lent itself naturally to myth. "The Japanese must have mountains of gold to be so independent," said the rumors. And so the raiders came.

KUBLAI KHAN COMES TO PLUNDER

The Mongol warlord Kublai Khan (grandson of Genghis Khan) was among the first, around 1274. He intended to make Japan a glorious addition to his empire. What happened next became the basis of legend—the first sure sign that Japan was a divine nation favored by the gods.

Kublai Khan ordered the Shogunate governors to surrender to him and declare Japan to be subject to Mongol rule. The governors refused. The story goes that Khan sent hundreds of ships and 20,000 soldiers to attack the mainland. The small army of Japanese defenders and samurai warriors fought against overwhelming odds and succeeded in driving the Mongols back to their ships to prepare for battle the next day. That night, the people of Japan sat trembling in their houses, waiting for the inevitable defeat and praying that they would not be enslaved at the hands of the barbarians.

Something cataclysmic happened; no one even now is exactly sure what. The seemingly safe harbor where the Mongols rested in their warships was battered by a massive storm that swept up the coast during the night. The howling winds tossed the invader ships into a fury of confusion, sinking hundreds and driving hundreds more into ruin. The next morning, when the wind died down, the Mongols saw they had little left to fight with and limped out of the harbor. It was a stunning turn of events that no one could quite believe.

A year later, Kublai had become one of the founding rulers of a new dynasty in China and sent his envoys to try to establish peaceful and lucrative trade with the fierce island nation. The Japanese unceremoniously chopped off the heads of the envoys. So much for peace.

Seven years later, Kublai Khan, demonstrating how serious he was this time, returned with a force six times the size of the first one—120,000 Mongol and Chinese fighters (so the story goes) and a fleet of 4,400 ships that filled the horizon. Once again the seemingly unstoppable Mongols battered the coast and tangled with the Japanese army. But now the defenders were stronger and smarter. Their forts were taller. Their swords were sharper. Once again, as darkness fell, the invaders retreated to their ships and anchored off to the southwest, where they rested for up to six weeks.

The emperor prayed to the gods for all his people, and sat down to wait for the next wave of barbarians.

And here, near the micro-island of Takashima, a typhoon whirled into the fleet on July 30. The ships had been chained together for safety in case the Japanese defenders decided to attack. But the chains made them vulnerable to the storm's fury.

The typhoon raged up the coast and trapped the enemy ships in a maelstrom of wind and rain and waves. When the first light of dawn shone on the scene, the wreckage of ships and drowned men was beyond describing—one of the largest sea disasters in history. (Three centuries later, in almost the exact same circumstances, the Spanish fleet of King Philip II was destroyed in a storm while attempting to conquer Elizabeth I and the English people with a force that would have certainly changed the course of history. The English, like the Japanese before them, took the storm as a sign of God's favor.)

In gratitude, the Japanese coined a new phrase to commemorate their salvation: Divine wind. It was the name they would give to their airplane pilots, seven centuries later, as they steered their bomb-laden fighter planes into the gray ships of the American navy in sea battles at places such as the Coral Sea and Midway Island, riding the wind directly onto the flight decks of the great aircraft carriers. The people knew in their hearts that for all of human history the sun would always rise on a victorious Japan.

Kublai maintained a strong (if foolish) desire to make Japan part of his empire and planned several more invasions. However, he had larger battles to fight elsewhere. When he died, in 1294, the Japanese at last began to believe that they were safe from foreign invasion.

Even today, local fishermen in Imari Bay will snag and pull up an artifact from those ancient battles: iron swords, stone spearheads, and cantaloupe-sized bombs used in catapult machines. Recently explorers have found a personal bronze seal of a thirteenth-century Mongol commander, as well as a 270-foot ship that almost certainly originated in Chinese Mongolia.

It seems the "kama kazi" (divine wind) was based in fact after all.

THE SAMURAI SPIRIT IMBUES JAPANESE CORPORATIONS

School children from Singapore to Seattle have heard the whispery legends of Japan's elite swordfighters. In the same way that the cowboy, in history and in myth, has shaped American culture, the truth and legend of the samurai warrior has deeply influenced the way that Japanese people think of themselves and of their place in the world community. The samurai swordsman, like the cowboy, holds his personal honor above all other considerations, tends to fight for vengeance or for the underdog, and carries within his lonely existence a personalized code of justice. He knows that he will not prevail in the end. He knows that history will pass him by—that his personal code will make him an outsider in polite and law-based society. Nevertheless, he will not change his ways because he cannot change his nature.

"Samurai" comes from the word *saburau,* "to serve." The true warrior served not himself but his sovereign lord, from whose glory the warrior himself derived a measure of respect and honor. The samurai alone were allowed to carry two swords—a distinction that clearly separated the fighters as a class from all other people.

The two swords varied in length. The longest, the *katana,* has a three-foot blade and an elegant handle, about 10 or 11 inches, woven of cotton or leather.

The short sword, or *wakizashi,* has a blade of about 18 inches and a shorter handle.

Both weapons are slightly curved, and wickedly sharp. The curve is designed to add greater force when a fighter slashes with it than he could achieve with a straight blade. Some swords have a "blood" groove, and some are flat.

The *katana* is designed for open field fighting, to achieve great slashing speed and to enable the fighter to maim or even behead his opponent with one or two lightning-fast movements. The *wakizashi* is a side weapon, to be used for in-close fighting where the samurai uses more wrist strength than arm strength.

Like so many other things Japanese (ancestor memorials, the tea ceremony, rock gardens, kabuki theater), samurai sword warfare is highly choreographed and ritualized.

First, the swords themselves are objects of great beauty and shimmering danger. Making and restoring them are highly prized arts in Japan. The metal is refined to an astonishing purity and sharpened to a lethal edge that swords made of lesser metals cannot hope to achieve. The pommels are artistically wrapped or wound or otherwise shaped to fit the hand magically. There are names for each element of the sword, and names for each manipulation of it against an enemy.

More on Swords and Swordsmanship

If you have an interest in samurai swords, here are some reference works for you:

- Gregory Irvine, *The Japanese Sword: The Soul of the Samurai* (Victoria & Albert, 2000).
- Setsuo Takaiwa et al., *The Art of Japanese Sword Polishing* (Kodansha International, 2006).
- Leon Kapp et al., *Modern Japanese Swords and Swordsmiths: From 1868 to the Present* (Kodansha International, 2002).

Several authorities, including the novelist Stephen Hunter, suggest that there are eight basic moves in samurai swordplay:

1. *Tsuki:* thrust
2. *Migi yokogiri:* side cut left to right
3. *Hidari yokogiri:* side cut right to left
4. *Migi kesagiri:* diagonal cut right to left
5. *Hidari kesagiri:* diagonal cut left to right
6. *Migi kiriage:* rising diagonal cut from right to left

7. *Hidari kiriage:* rising diagonal cut from left to right
8. *Shinchokugiri:* vertical downward

Second, although sword fighting has some of the aspects of a dance about it, make no mistake: It is deadly serious business. The swords are so cunningly sharp that they easily lop off limbs or open up a torso. The people who wield them are brave and athletic.

As the samurai life began to wane in the seventeenth century, the warriors themselves began to codify their activities into an expression of the ideal: *bushido* (the warrior's way). The best-known by far of all the samurai stories is called "The 47 *Ronin.*" A *ronin*, or wanderer, was a samurai who had been permanently separated from his lord, whether by death or war. As Japan's medieval period came to a close, the countryside started to fill up with these homeless wanderers. They were nomads because they had no skill save the sword, no means of supporting themselves save fighting, and no family save their master's household, now dissolved. The famous story about the 47 *Ronin* came to stand for a distillation of all samurai virtues.

In 1701, Lord Asano Naganori had been insulted by the Shogun's right-hand man, Kira Yoshinaka, in front of the Shogun and his family. In response, Asano drew his sword and was quickly condemned to death for such an act of arrogance in the Shogun's castle. He was forced to commit *seppuku,* the deliberate self-disemboweling achieved by cutting open one's abdomen in prescribed and ritualized motions. The Shogun appropriated Asano's family home and expelled 47 of his faithful samurai. The 47 vowed to kill Kira and hid their intent behind a façade of drinking and loose living for many months. As time went by, Kira and his supporters relaxed their watchfulness.

One day, Kira, suspecting nothing, lounged in his house unguarded. The *ronin* slashed their way through the house's walls and set upon him like wolves on a lamb. They offered to let him commit *seppuku* himself, but he was too cowardly. So they cut off his head in disrespect and put it on Asano's grave. For this act they were widely praised by the people—and also condemned by the authorities. While their act was a clear example of *bushido,* the samurai were ordered to kill themselves in a mass act of *seppuku.*

They were buried at a site near the Sengakuji Temple in Tokyo; their graves are now a major tourist attraction.

In modern times the *ronin* warrior culture was celebrated in a 1954 film called *The Seven Samurai,* starring Toshiro Mifune, about seven swordsmen who are hired by farmers to protect their homes and crops from bandits. If this sounds familiar, the same plot was later Americanized in *The Magnificent Seven,* starring Yul Brynner and Steve McQueen. The connection made in the two films between samurai warriors and cowboy gunslingers was clear and inevitable, as it was in the remake of the Japanese director

Akira Kurosawa's film *Yojimbo,* called a *Fistful of Dollars* in the version starring Clint Eastwood.

JAPAN TIGHTENS ITS BORDERS

Until Commodore Perry showed up with his famous guns, most foreign visitors to Japan had been rudely repulsed or even more rudely executed. Japanese rulers were particularly anxious that Catholic Christian missionaries make no inroads into their culture of easygoing Buddhism. Tattletales in every village kept an eye on things, ever watchful for the random crucifix hanging on a wall or a peasant falling onto his knees to pray.

While the entire Pacific Rim was opening to foreign trade and influence, Japan was putting locks on its doors.

Russia knocked on those doors in 1792 and tried again in 1804. Great Britain was a constant nuisance, as were the American merchant and whaling vessels that were eternally looking for supplies and a friendly port. Japan looked at how Western influences had corrupted China, with its opium dens and debased cities, and vowed to have nothing to do with the Western outsiders. Meanwhile, within the walls, any Japanese citizen who urged opening the country to foreign trade was punished, imprisoned—or worse. For example, Sakuma Shozan, who coined the slogan "Eastern Ethics, Western Science," was murdered.

Against this background, Matthew Perry (1794–1858) majestically steamed into Tokyo Bay. He carried with him an official request for three improvements:

1. Treat castaways who float up to Japan's shores more humanely.
2. Open Japanese ports of call to supplies and coal.
3. Open the gates wide for trade.

After the Emperor's representatives allowed him to cool his heels for a few days, they finally agreed to a face-to-face meeting. The Commodore (who writes about himself in the third person) writes at length about the encounter. Here are some excerpts, in the flowery style of Perry's day.

Ornamental screens of cloth...had been stretched tightly in the usual way upon posts of wood...Upon these seeming panels were emblazoned the imperial arms, alternating with the device of a scarlet flower bearing large heart-shaped leaves. Flags and streamers, upon which were various designs represented in gay colors, hung from the several angles of the screens, while behind them thronged crowds of soldiers, arrayed in a costume which had not been before observed, and which was supposed to belong to high occasions only. The main portion of the dress was a species of frock of a dark color, with short skirts, the waists of which were gathered in with a sash, and which was without sleeves, the arms of the wearers being bare.

All on board the ships were alert from the earliest hour.... Steam was got up and the anchors were weighed that the ships might be moved to a position where their guns would command the place of reception.... The officers, seamen, and marines who were to accompany the Commodore were selected, and as large a number of them mustered as could possibly be spared from the whole squadron. All, of course, were eager to bear a part in the ceremonies of the day.... Many of the officers and men were selected by lot, and when the full complement, which amounted to nearly three hundred, was filled up, each one busied himself in getting his person ready for the occasion. The officers, as had been ordered, were in full official dress, while the sailors and marines were in their naval and military uniforms of blue and white....

From the beginning the two [Japanese] princes had assumed an air of statuesque formality, which they preserved during the whole interview, as they never spoke a word, and rose from their seats only at the entrance and exit of the Commodore, when they made a grave and formal bow...

The letter of the President, Millard Fillmore, expressed the friendly feelings of the United States toward Japan and his desire that there should be friendship and trade between the two countries. The documents were laid upon the scarlet box and a formal receipt was given for them....

The procession re-formed as before, and the Commodore was escorted to his barge, and, embarking, was rowed off toward his ship, followed by the other American and the two Japanese boats which contained the Governor of Uraga and his attendants, the bands meanwhile playing our national airs with great spirit as the boats pulled off to the ships.

In addition to the request (backed up by heavy cannon), Perry left behind a letter from the President and a thoughtful gift of a number of white flags, to make surrender easier. Then he steamed away, promising to return soon.

Mr. Fillmore's letter was several pages long, and in the delicate language of diplomacy. Here are some excerpts:

I am desirous that our two countries should trade with each other, for the benefit both of Japan and the United States.... We know that the ancient laws of your imperial majesty's government do not allow of foreign trade, except with the Chinese and the Dutch; but as the state of the world changes and new governments are formed, it seems to be wise, from time to time, to make new laws....

Our steamships, in crossing the great ocean, burn a great deal of coal, and it is not convenient to bring it all the way from America. We wish that our steamships and other vessels should be allowed to stop in Japan and supply themselves with coal, provisions, and water. They will pay for them in money, or anything else your imperial majesty's subjects may prefer; and we request your imperial majesty to appoint a convenient port, in the southern part of the Empire, where our vessels may stop for this purpose. We are very desirous of this.

These are the only objects for which I have sent Commodore Perry, with a powerful squadron, to pay a visit to your imperial majesty's renowned city of Yedo [now Tokyo]: friendship, commerce, a supply of coal and provisions, and protection for our shipwrecked people....May the Almighty have your imperial majesty in His great and holy keeping!...

Your good friend, Millard Fillmore

Within the government there was turmoil, as well as a growing acquiescence to the inevitability of the "world" crashing in on Japan's private party.

Perry returned early in 1854 with nine ships this time—more than enough to make a big impression. The Shogunate signed the Treaty of Kanagawa of March 1854, granting for the first time the desire of the Americans to open up an ambassador's post in Edo. It was subsequently moved to the coastal city of Shimoda in 1856.

After the Americans had broken down the doors to trade, there was little point in holding back. Treaties quickly followed with Great Britain, Holland, France, and Russia. Japan was now a vital part of the international maritime community of nations.

Even so, the people understood that they were set apart by the gods for glorious achievements. In the quiet of their own hearts, every Japanese man, woman, and child could still hear the divine wind.

CHANGES COME

The next job for Japanese political leaders was to open up the country for modernization by easing the stranglehold of the culture on the rigid class system.

About the time of the American Civil War, the class system in Japan was restructured to allow for growing development and international trade. Ancient restrictions on the kind of work each class could do were erased. The class system itself was eased and broadened into less-clear strata:

- *Kozoku* (imperial family)
- *Kazoku* (nobility)

- *Shizoku* (samurai)
- *Heimin* (common people).

The leaders formed a new government, named *Meiji* (enlightened rule) after the new emperor. The earlier shoguns had diminished the role of the emperor while elevating their own status and the power of the samurai. Now all that was changing. New local ministers came into power and restored to the emperor what they believed was his rightful heritage as a supreme ruler blessed by the gods. These ministers also saw themselves as ones who spoke for the emperor and assumed great control for themselves over all civilian activities, through World War II.

Similarly, military leaders were groomed to provide Japan with a bellicose culture that so obviously would be needed if Japan were to assume equal status among nations with long-standing armies and navies. These enterprising officers designed and built military academies whose hallmark was a rigid hierarchy and absolute obedience to the authorities centralized in Edo, soon to be Tokyo. If Japan must compete on the world stage, it would compete to win.

By 1870, under loosening traditions, peasants had begun to give themselves surnames. Meanwhile, many other ancient ways were yielding to the demands of modernity. The traditional stipend system for samurai, for example, was gradually phased out. They were expected to find their own gainful employment, often as village administrators or government and military functionaries. In 1876, all samurai were prohibited from wearing swords. There was no longer any room for men of the sword and the knife in the new world.

The age of the swordfighter was over; the age of the merchant had begun.

At some point almost certainly after 1870, a family clan of commoners that had been rice farmers for generations decided to acknowledge the nutrient-rich crop that had sustained them for so long by giving themselves a new and respectful surname: Toyoda.

Growing and harvesting rice had provided the Toyoda clan with a living, but not with prosperity. It would take a man of extraordinary courage and rare ambition to lead the clan from its Stone Age existence into the modern world. Ever since Commodore Perry had materialized like a magician's trick in their harbor with the political will and the weapons systems of modern technology, Japanese people with vision and imagination had understood that it would take more than desire for Japan to assume a place among the decision makers and entrepreneurs and adventurers of the world.

It would take engineers.

Chapter Two

The Founders

We are going to meet some people in this chapter whose brilliance and hard work was directly responsible for the global success of Toyota Motor Corporation. Just how that company became a world-changing enterprise is a complex story that will take several chapters to unfold.

Whoever the first people to carry the family name were, it is certain they were farmers for generations, scratching a living from the same small plot of land, with its intricate paddy system, and surrounded by small, jagged mountains and bamboo groves.

The family name, Toyoda, means "abundant rice fields."

Arms of a Conglomerate

The modern Toyota Group encompasses the following companies, in order of their founding:

1. Toyoda Boshoku Co., Ltd. Founded January 1918. (In November 1943, it merged with Toyota Motor Company. It became independent again in May 1950, as Minsei Spinning Co., Ltd. The organization changed its name to Toyoda Boshoku Company in August 1967 and merged with Toyota Kako Company, Ltd., in October 2000.)
2. Toyoda Automatic Loom Works, Ltd., founded in November 1926. It is now called Toyota Industries Company.
3. Toyota Motor Co., Ltd., founded in August 1937.
4. Aichi Steel Works, Ltd., founded in March 1940.
5. Toyoda Machine Works, Ltd., founded in May 1941.

IKICHI TOYODA'S SON LEAVES THE FARM

Ikichi (ee-KEY-chee) Toyoda (toy-o-DAH) was a rice farmer, as was his father and his father before him and back through the mists of time. In most of the sparse accounts of Ikichi, he is also called a "poor carpenter."

Like most poor people, he worked long hours at several occupations. The clan lived in the small village of Yamaguchi, in present-day Kosai, Shizuoka, Japan, only a few hundred miles from Tokyo but isolated from all the political and cultural changes that were fermenting in that great city.

Ikichi and his family lived on the same small plot of land that had supported his ancestors. The land did not produce much, but they were not starving. Ikichi evidently added to his family's meager income by carpentry work, at which he must have been quite skilled. At any rate, he is the first of the Toyoda line to be called anything but a peasant farmer. Some accounts term him "self-confident" and "strong-minded." In that culture, those terms were not necessarily approving. Obedience was highly prized, as was modesty and an awareness of one's station. To aspire to anything grander took great courage.

Just a few months before the Meiji throne was restored to rule Japan, Sakichi Toyoda (sa-KEE-chee), son of Ikichi, was born. April 14, 1867, was undoubtedly a soft spring day in the foothills of the sharp, tooth-shaped mountains, and it was undoubtedly a fine occasion for the whole village, whose reliance on producing new generations of farmers was traditional.

Ikichi Toyoda, being an honorable Japanese man and the honored head of his household, passed many of his traditions on to his eldest son. Like many tribal societies, the villagers saw eldest sons as carriers of the clan's history and the creators of its future. Ikichi expected his son to fall in line, to accept his fate and his place, to honor his father above all and his family next. In any family, the eldest male was the final arbiter in all things. His approval was to be sought in every major decision, for without it no changes would be made. He was expected to be wise and courageous in all things, and to pass on those qualities to his eldest son. And so on. Forever.

There are stories that Sakichi worked with his father on carpentry projects after school. Like most carpenter apprentices, he undoubtedly learned the value of doing what works, rather than what is theoretical. Most accounts of his early life suggest that he was not all that interested in carpentry, and certainly not at all interested in farming. Nevertheless, the value of precision, of doing it right the first time, of measuring and measuring and measuring, must have become clear to his young mind.

We may see the boy, after completing a few years of the only education he could reasonably expect to have, leaving the house before dawn with his father, the strap of the heavy toolbox cutting into his small shoulder, a tiny bamboo box of rice inside the toolbox for his lunch. His father would walk ahead briskly, perhaps sharing news with the other artisans and farmers they met along the way, the boy always dragging slightly behind and always trying to keep up. The father would be certain and sure of his place in his world; the son would be worried that this might be the only life he would ever know.

The tenets of Confucianism, in which Ikichi must certainly have believed, required that a father demand absolute obedience from his son, because such behavior was good for the son and good for the clan. Sakichi, for his part, was less than an ideal son in the Japanese tradition. He tended to daydream. He found little of interest in the precise cutting of wood or in the muck of rice paddies. He felt he was destined for more than this, and he feared that everyone felt the same way and that he was ordinary after all.

While almost certainly strict in the Japanese tradition of fathers, Ikichi would have passed on his ambition and his skill with tools—and, maybe best of all, the tools themselves—to his eldest son, with whom the story of the great Toyota Motor Corporation really begins.

Looking back on the early lives of people who achieve greatness, we often assume that those individuals somehow intuit the glory that lies ahead of them and so take the steps to make that glory happen. The reality, however, is that the individual, often young, often in poor circumstances and despairing of ever making something of his or her life, simply acts out of sheer courage. Achieving great things is an act of will. And so they step off into the future, often rejecting their past and their families, in favor of the greatest gamble of their lives.

Sakichi was to become a national hero—an entrepreneur, a visionary, an inventor, a tinkerer, a believer in practical experimentation over impractical theory, a craftsman, and a founder of a magnificent corporation that would help restore Japan after the devastation of a world war. Many years after his death in 1930, the Japanese patent office would name Sakichi Toyoda as one of the most important inventors in all of Japanese history. Given the far-ranging impact of his contributions, he is certainly one of the most important inventors in world history as well, worthy to be named in the same breath as Thomas Edison and Eli Whitney.

But for now he is just a boy, living with his family on a little piece of land that bears a rice crop year after year.

Historians are tempted to imbue the early years of any famous person—especially one with poor beginnings—with a warm glow of sentiment. Abraham Lincoln, for example, has long been celebrated as the backwoods rail-splitter who read books by the light of burning logs. But even Lincoln himself groaned at the memory of the hard work and calloused palms and rough-cloth jackets that marked him forever as a bumpkin among sophisticated Washington, D.C., society. Anyone who has ever split fireplace logs with an ax even for an hour knows the despair that sets in as the muscles begin to ache and the pile of unsplit wood seems to grow bigger.

Similarly, Sakichi was a precocious boy who could look ahead and see nothing but backbreaking work in the paddies for the rest of his days, drenched in the rainy season and parched in the dry months, surrounded by thirsty mosquitoes, and oppressed by the needs of a growing family that looked to him for its only source of food.

From what he himself said about those early years, it was his mother's money-making sideline as a weaver, as well as a timely government regulation, that changed his life.

In 1885, the Meiji government enacted the "Regulations of Special Permit of Patent" to protect new inventions and encourage entrepreneurship. This was new thinking in Japan. Previously, working for the common good of all was assumed to drive the inventive spirit. But devoting precious time and effort to developing new things—when you could be resting up for the next day's labor in the rice fields—required a belief that such sacrifice would lead to personal gain. It required a *capitalistic* spirit, which is hard to come by in a communal society where one should never work to stand out or be noticed as an individual.

Recognizing that self-interest is the most powerful motivator of all, the regulators issued the new rules just in time for a bright young inventor to take advantage of them. And it was the second most powerful motivator—love for one's family—that led Sakichi Toyoda in the direction that would alter history.

Weaving had been a part of Japanese peasant life since the beginning of the clans. As in most primitive societies, men and boys concentrated on hunting and building tasks; women and girls did the cooking and weaving. When the hunting was no longer plentiful or productive, men turned to growing food in the fields, and women concentrated on weaving cloth. Every home in Sakichi's village had a simple handmade and hand-operated loom. It took a full day of hard work to produce just a yard of cloth. There was nothing smooth about this material. It was rough, uneven, and coarse to the touch, almost like burlap. The fibers were stiff and unyielding. But the material would serve for a farmer's clothing and could reasonably keep a worker somewhat dry in poor weather.

A woman who was proficient at the loom could make more cloth than her household needed and so could sell the extra material to neighbors or to other villagers at the local market. It was one of the few ways a farmer's wife could contribute actual income to the family. A woman of unusual skill as a weaver could produce finer versions of this rough cloth, which would mean that her surplus cloth would sell first in the market and that she could command the best prices for it. Sakichi Toyoda's mother was such a woman.

Unfortunately, Commodore Perry's success at opening up Japan to the world's trade was now having a direct, negative impact on Madame Toyoda's ability to sell her rough fabrics. Shiploads of goods from Great Britain, Portugal, Spain, even China and other Pacific Rim countries were finding their way into Japanese markets for the first time. And, for the first time, Japanese customers were discovering that homemade fabrics were shockingly disappointing when compared to the smooth and elegant cloth of Western weavers. Western cotton fabrics were durable, of course, like their Japanese counterparts. But, unlike them, they were deliciously supple to the touch and able to hold bright colors for much longer than the rough cloth from Japanese villages. It was as if Japan's women weavers were suddenly thrust onto a world stage that was a hundred years ahead of them. Holding samples of the two fabrics in either hand, the weavers could see that they could not possibly compete with the quality of the Western cloth. If they sold their own rough cloth at all, it would be at rock-bottom prices.

To add salt to the wound, the friendly merchants who used to buy cloth from the village women stopped coming around altogether. The bottom had dropped out of an already tentative income-producing sideline. The West, with its industrialized, coal-fired weaving factories and highly trained workers and urban centers rich with raw material, was simply too far ahead. Even adding shipping costs to the imported cloth, the Western fabrics were so well and so cheaply made that manufacturers could underprice the village goods and still make a profit.

Japanese weavers would have to drastically improve the quality of their cloth and triple or quadruple the speed of production or else burn the looms for firewood and resign themselves to poverty forever.

Sakichi Toyoda had enough confidence in his inventive skills to believe that he could help Japanese women compete with the West—but it would take looms that were light-years ahead of the one his mother was using.

So Sakichi started tinkering just at the exact time when the government started to encourage such a thing for the first time in Japanese history. The great revolution in industry was flowing across the land, and Sakichi found himself in the first wave.

More precisely, he found himself in the first classroom.

In 1885, Sakichi and his fellow schoolmates from Yamaguchi attended a lecture by a teacher from the new government in Tokyo. The teacher looked them all in the eyes and explained that the old ways of the fathers and grandfathers were no longer working. The samurai were gone. The passing of land from one generation to the next was no longer enough. Farming was fine for peasants who had nowhere to go and nothing to accomplish. But the newly arrived Western culture had brought with it a grand awakening—a realization that Japan must compete with builders and inventors and adventurers and merchants from across the sea who were far ahead of these village boys. Young men from the West were inventing steamships and building canals and forging steel and erecting cities, while Japanese boys were making do with a meager portion of rice for lunch. Kublai Khan, with his armies and fire-flinging ships, could not bring down this great island nation. But international commerce could. Japan must rise to meet this newest and greatest challenge or else be abandoned by the gods and blown away on an economic—not divine—wind.

Sakichi looked around at his fellows and saw a variety of reactions. Some were awed and afraid of this thing the teacher was calling "technology" and "commerce." Some were sad and bitter as they realized that the old ways were changing forever. And some, like Sakichi, were filled with a fearful ambition to absorb the truth of what the teacher was saying and to create great things out of their meager resources.

The government would help, the teacher told the boys. The government would register patents and protect the financial interests of the patent holder. What was formerly held in common would now be held by the individual who made it. A nation of farmers and mud movers would become a nation of industrial visionaries.

Sakichi now found his heart filled with this frightening new ambition, and he resolved that he would be a farmer or a carpenter no longer but an inventor who would lead his family and his country into a new industrialized future. Like the young Abraham Lincoln, who was too poor to buy books and too poor to afford candles in order to read borrowed books, Sakichi knew he must build greatness out of nothing. When he returned home from the classroom that evening, he saw his mother's antique and recalcitrant loom standing in the corner.

Timeline of Sakichi Toyoda's Life

1867	Born into a poor family of farmers and carpenters
1887	Starts working on designing better looms
1890	Travels to Tokyo for Third National Industrial Exhibition
1891	Patents his first loom
1894	Kiichiro is born
1895	Founds Toyoda Company to sell yarn-reeling machines
1896	Marries his second wife after divorcing the first
1899	Signs a 10-year agreement with Mitsui & Company for rights to his power loom
1904	Russian-Japanese War begins; economy improves
1907	Dissolves Toyoda Company, creates Toyoda Loom Works
1912	Creates Toyoda Automatic Weaving Company. It becomes Toyoda Spinning & Weaving Company
1914	World War I creates economic boom
1926	Founds Toyoda Automatic Loom Works
1930	Dies of pneumonia on October 30

Later in life, Sakichi said that during this period he was fortunate to come across a book by a British author, titled *Self-Help*. The book had just come out in a Japanese translation and was an instant hit. The author, Samuel Smiles (1812–1904), wrote about how certain individuals across history's landscape had overcome odds that would have overwhelmed lesser men.

"The spirit of self-help," Smiles said, "is the root of all genuine growth in the individual; and, exhibited in the lives of many, it constitutes the true source of national vigour and strength." When Sakichi read that for the first time, he may have been thinking of the divine wind that tore through the fleet of Kublai Khan. His nation's "vigour and strength" were things that Sakichi yearned for every day, just as he yearned to be among those who restored them to his beloved Japan.

Smiles wrote about the Puritan ethic and how it had helped to shape and harden these successful people so that nothing could stand in their way. He described the virtues of self-reliance, of belief in a divine being or destiny, of a proper kind of pride that allowed one to enjoy the fruits of success that came from following one's own sense of rightness.

It is difficult to overemphasize the impact of Samuel Smiles on Sakichi. It is the only book on display at Sakichi's birthplace; Sakichi carried it with him the way divinity students carry the Bible, and he carefully marked passages for later pondering. It may not be too much to suggest that Samuel Smiles is the philosophical godfather of today's Toyota.

Like a British version of Ben Franklin, Smiles doted on the memorable aphorism. And, like Franklin, Smiles continually underscored the overwhelming authority of time. Almost everything else in life is replaceable; time is the one commodity that can be lost forever and never recovered. That truth was to become the central tenet of the Toyoda family's search for perfection.

The student of Toyota can find numerous verbal nuggets that became buried in Toyota's many rules for success. In an early passage in *Self-Help* Smiles provides a haunting foundation for Sakichi's business style:

> The spirit of self-help, as exhibited in the energetic action of individuals, has in all times been a marked feature in the English character, and furnishes the true measure of our power as a nation. Rising above the heads of the mass, there were always to be found a series of individuals distinguished beyond others, who commanded the public homage. But our progress has also been owing to multitudes of smaller and less known men. Though only the generals' names may be remembered in the history of any great campaign, it has been in a great measure through the individual valour and heroism of the privates that victories have been won.
>
> And life, too, is "a soldiers' battle,"—men in the ranks having in all times been amongst the greatest of workers. Many are the lives of men unwritten, which have nevertheless as powerfully influenced civilisation and progress as the more fortunate Great whose names are recorded in biography. Even the humblest person, who

sets before his fellows an example of industry, sobriety, and upright honesty of purpose in life, has a present as well as a future influence upon the well-being of his country; for his life and character pass unconsciously into the lives of others, and propagate good example for all time to come.

Where the Scotsman Smiles saw Puritans in their black clothing and stern faces, Sakichi Toyoda saw samurai.

The samurai warrior looked nowhere for help. He followed his own code. He stood or fell according to his own lights. He followed a master but was no slave. He did not fear death or anything other men could do to him. He feared only failure.

Sakichi Toyoda would be a new kind of samurai. He would follow the path that he himself created. He knew he could do it. And he knew one other thing just as certainly: His father would never approve.

The son, now just 18 years old, made an important decision in his mind. He would reject the demands of his father and his clan. He would not spend his life bending over rice plants. He would not saw and hammer houses and animal carts and benches for extra pay. He would invent grand things, and he would bring glory to his family and to his newly energized nation.

And so Sakichi Toyoda turned his full attention to making his mother's loom not just better, but a miracle of engineering invention.

The Wisdom of Samuel Smiles
- A place for everything, and everything in its place.
- An intense anticipation itself transforms possibility into reality; our desires being often but precursors of the things which we are capable of performing.
- Enthusiasm . . . the sustaining power of all great action.
- He who never made a mistake never made a discovery.
- Hope is the companion of power, and mother of success; for who so hopes strongly has within him the gift of miracles.
- It is a mistake to suppose that men succeed through success; they much oftener succeed through failures. Precept, study, advice, and example could never have taught them so well as failure has done.
- It is energy—the central element of which is will—that produces the miracle that is enthusiasm in all ages. Everywhere it is what is called force of character and the sustaining power of all great action.
- Knowledge conquered by labor becomes a possession—a property entirely our own.

- Labor is still, and ever will be, the inevitable price set upon everything which is valuable.
- Lost wealth may be replaced by industry, lost knowledge by study, lost health by temperance or medicine, but lost time is gone forever.
- Men who are resolved to find a way for themselves will always find opportunities enough; and if they do not find them, they will make them.
- Practical wisdom is only to be learned in the school of experience. Precepts and instruction are useful so far as they go, but, without the discipline of real life, they remain of the nature of theory only.
- Progress, of the best kind, is comparatively slow. Great results cannot be achieved at once; and we must be satisfied to advance in life as we walk, step by step.
- The apprenticeship of difficulty is one which the greatest of men have had to serve.
- The experience gathered from books, though often valuable, is but the nature of learning, whereas the experience gained from actual life is one of the nature of wisdom.
- The spirit of self-help is the root of all genuine growth in the individual.
- The very greatest things—great thoughts, discoveries, inventions—have usually been nurtured in hardship, often pondered over in sorrow, and at length established with difficulty.
- Wisdom and understanding can only become the possession of individual men by traveling the old road of observation, attention, perseverance, and industry.

Samuel Smiles, *Self-Help*
(The Echo Library, 2006).

THE BASICS OF WEAVING

A weaver interlaces two or more sets of thread, usually at right angles to each other, to create a tight compaction that has myriad uses, from shedding water to holding warmth. The trick is the thread. Rough thread is the easiest to weave but the least pleasant to use and to wear. The silkier a thread is, the more it pleases the wearer and the more it drives the weaver to distraction. Fine thread has a mind of its own and must be rigidly controlled. But it is like controlling spider webs.

The loom is a clever device that aids in interlacing the material into textile, or fabric. Looms range from portable, hand-held wooden frames to large frames pegged into the ground to immense industrial machines capable of interweaving hundreds of separate threads and colors.

Let's say that, like Sakichi's mother, you are holding a wooden loom on your lap. It is like holding a wood picture frame, with the north/south dimension about twice as long as the east/west dimension. The threads running north/south from you are arranged in parallel rows tightly together. They are the *warp* threads, and they are under strong tension. The *weft* threads run left and right across your frame. They begin loose and—once intertwined with the warp threads—are tightened and pressed together.

You use your hand or a wooden pin—called a *shuttle*—to weave the weft threads in and out among the warp threads. The earliest weavers simply raised and lowered every warp thread one at a time while they weaved in the weft threads. Even today, kindergarten students make "potholders" this way to the joy of their parents. This is mind-numbing work when done on an industrial scale.

Serious weaving requires that the weft thread or shuttle push through alternate warp threads at the same time. This requires a mechanical raising and lowering of the warp while the weft is simultaneously passed through and packed down. Even describing it is complicated. Doing it is an immense challenge. As we shall see in the next chapter, Sakichi's success at designing and manufacturing state-of-the-art looms formed the foundation for the world-dominating enterprise known as the Toyota Motor Corporation.

The carpenter Ikichi Toyoda had two sons after Sakichi: Sasuke, and Heikichi (1875–1954), who was the father of Eiji Toyoda, who would be president of Toyota Motor Corporation in the modern world. Sakichi's eldest son was Kiichiro Toyoda (1894–1952), who directly founded Toyota Motor Corporation.

KIICHIRO TOYODA: LIKE FATHER, LIKE SON

My father was a loom man. I'm an automobile man.

—Kiichiro Toyoda

All cultures in all eras tell the same story, enhanced in the modern age by the insights of Sigmund Freud. A son must first separate himself from his mother. He is, after all, male and not female. He learns early that he does not share his mother's concerns or her way of looking at the world. Then he must separate himself from his father. He yearns to make his own way in the world, to be his own man and not just his father's son. It is a tension that drives history, and the Toyoda family is no exception.

Kiichiro knew early on that he didn't want to be like his father. It was an ironic twist of the "just desserts" variety, for Sakichi knew the same truth about his own father. Once again the son would disappoint and embarrass the father, and once again the father would come to see his son as an achiever greater than himself.

Soon after this birth, Sakichi Toyoda divorced his wife, Kiichiro's mother. Sakichi was away from home tinkering and inventing while Kiichiro was young; the boy had little or no contact with his father, and the absence had a negative impact on the boy. While Kiichiro was still quite young, he went to live with his blended family, consisting of his father, his stepmother, Asako, and his half-sister, Aiko. Since both parents worked, Kiichiro was left to his own devices much of the time. He seemed to brood and draw inward. He resisted his stepmother's authority over him and seemed to resent his father for leaving him under Asako's stern thumb. In spite of their differences, however, Asako insisted that the boy continue his education even beyond the required elementary school. Kiichiro was an indifferent student, to the exasperation of both parents.

As we'll see in the next chapter, by this time Sakichi had become a success. His looms had started to find a market in the wider world. They were competing with the great loom companies of Europe and bringing in rivers of cash for the first time. Toyoda was no longer a rice farmer's name; it was an entrepreneur's name, the signature of an inventor and businessman. Given his father's newly acquired wealth and stature in the business community, Kiichiro went to a good, expensive school, where he was immediately tagged as a farmer's son who was committing the sin of trying to better himself. Kiichiro made no friends at school. His country ways and lack of sophistication branded him an upstart and an outsider. He turned instead to expanding his interests in machinery.

Meanwhile, Sakichi's business interests were mounting. He cared little for managing other people and worrying about such mundane matters as profit and loss. He was an inventor and wanted to get back to what he loved. In a normal household in Japan, the father would pass on such management to his eldest son. Unfortunately, from Sakichi's point of view, Kiichiro was deeply ensconced in his own interests and had no desire to leave school to help his father. (The irony of this was almost certainly not lost on Sakichi, who had shown the same attitude toward his father, Ikichi.)

So Sakichi turned to a less traditional direction. His best friend and business associate, Ichizo Kodama, had helped Sakichi during several economic downturns. One day Sakichi mentioned to Kodama that his hopes for his son were not working out (the boy seemed to be an eternal student), and therefore he was looking for a husband for his daughter, Aiko, who was now of marriageable age. He thought that perhaps a new son-in-law would find the family spinning and loom business attractive. It was typical Japanese understatement. Any young man with common sense would have found the loom company to be a huge opportunity.

"As it turns out," Kodama said to Sakichi, "my younger brother Risaburo would be a perfect match for your company and for your daughter." Risaburo Kodama, at 31, was a successful manager of a cotton trading company, and he seemed like just the man Sakichi was looking for.

Sakichi, in the manner of Japanese fathers at the time, made up his mind on the spot that Risaburo was his choice for his daughter.

There was only one request he wanted to make. His businesses were strong and getting stronger. He had tried to bring in managers from outside the family to run things, and all attempts had failed. Since nothing was stronger than family, Sakichi would bring in Risaburo as his manager if Risaburo would agree to one thing: change his name to Toyoda and become Sakichi's adopted son. In Japan, this was not an unusual request. Risaburo was agreeable to this.

But no one thought to ask Kiichiro how *he* felt about it.

What Kiichiro felt most was betrayal. If Sakichi adopted Risaburo, then Risaburo would become the eldest son, subject to all the inheritance rights under Japanese law. Kiichiro naturally protested the adoption plan vigorously, but he was ignored, further deepening the division between himself and his father. After marrying Aiko, in 1915, Risaburo Kodama became Risaburo Toyoda.

RISABURO TOYODA: THE OUTSIDER COMES INSIDE

At the beginning of the twentieth century, if one were to paint a portrait of the Ideal Japanese Man, Risaburo could easily have been the model. Where Kiichiro was shy and self-effacing, Risaburo, 10 years older, was assertive and confident. He did not create—he managed others with a hard demeanor. He did not suggest—he gave orders. He cared little for machines or the little oiled intricacies that made them work—he demanded obedience to a plan and to his decisions.

As the new president of Toyoda Spinning & Weaving Company, the successful company that Sakichi had founded, Risaburo's mission was clear: to keep the company prosperous and growing for the benefit of the family and the glory of Japan.

However, it would be too easy to see Risaburo as the gray man who counted paper clips and ordered around staff and lacked imagination. As the putative eldest son, he had responsibilities he could not shirk. As the husband of Sakichi's beloved daughter and the brother of Sakichi's biological son, he had to walk a delicate line. That line became more like a shackle binding him to the company's fate in later years, when Kiichiro demanded more and more of the profits for his automobile researches and Aiko pressured him to help her brother no matter what cost.

Risaburo held to his honor throughout. He never unburdened his mind as to what he really thought of the arrangement that vaulted him ahead of Kiichiro in the family and in the business. He never complained about the pressures of business on the one side and the whining of relatives on the other. He remained faithful to the wishes of his adoptive father. He did always what he thought was right at the time, in circumstances in which a lesser man would have thrown up his hands and walked out the door.

The one thing everyone always recognized in Risaburo is that he was the consummate business professional who kept everything running. He was widely admired in Japanese business circles for his acumen and his rigid adherence to doing all things properly and in order. It was left up to the natural son to dream and fail, dream and fail, dream and fail and keep asking for more money. It was the adopted son's job to keep the profits of the loom business up while the natural son indulged in wild ideas about turning a loom factory into an automobile factory and demanded capital for his failed experiments in a corner of that factory.

No one has erected a statue to Risaburo for doing what was right virtually all the time, even when doing what was right impacted his own wishes and his own fortune. One erects statues to dreamers and adventurers, not to accountants. Risaburo was a steady holder of Kiichiro's coat while the younger man was off chasing his dream of a Japanese car to rival Detroit's products. Yet it is safe to surmise that there would be no Toyota Motor Company today if Risaburo had not been willing to abandon his own birth name and take on the mantle of the Toyoda family as it teetered on the edge, with bankruptcy on one side and wealth beyond dreams on the other.

Risaburo never imagined that he would outlive his adopted brother, but he did. Kiichiro died suddenly of a cerebral hemorrhage when he was only 57 years old. Risaburo died two months later, at 68, wracked by tuberculosis and struggling to breathe. Among his last words to Eiji Toyoda, the man who would steer Toyota into a worldwide reputation for excellence, was his final pronouncement on the family enterprise: "Whatever you do, have Toyota make cars."

All of that having been said, there was one truth that Risaburo took with him to his grave and never mentioned to anyone. It was perhaps the saddest of all truths in the family. When Sakichi, the maker of looms, old and frail at the end, looked across the Pacific at the success of American motor cars and first dared to dream that his own family could be mentioned in the same breath as the Ford family, it was to the ear of only one son that the old man whispered his dream: Kiichiro. It was Risaburo's lot in life to fund the dreams that enabled other family members to take Toyoda enterprises into the direction of automobiles. He seemed to understand that no one celebrates the moneylenders who sent Magellan across the oceans or Lewis and Clark to the Pacific shore. One can imagine him smiling at the praise given now to others for their foresight and cleverness. Risaburo had the one thing that made the family's future come true: He controlled the money.

EIJI TOYODA: THE QUIET MAN WHO GRASPED THE FUTURE

It is rare for the individual who starts a company to take it into a global future, and Toyota is no exception. Several earlier Toyoda men made the money and dreamed the dream and built the company. Eiji drove the company onto the world's stage.

Born in 1913, cousin to Kiichiro, he was a rightful blood member of the Toyoda clan. In taking over after Kiichiro's death, he bridged the successful Toyoda Automatic Loom Works and the Toyota Motor Corporation with his own vision of what it would take to achieve greatness.

Modest and unimposing in the traditional way of Japan, Eiji combined a fierce intelligence with the will to make things work.

"When I went to Detroit in 1950," he says, "we were producing forty cars a day. Ford was making eight-thousand units, a two-hundred-times difference. The gap was enormous" (Reingold, 1999).

He grew up, he says, in his father's textile mill near Nagoya. (Thanks to Sakichi, textiles had become the family business.) From his earliest childhood days, Eiji was involved with machinery and business ledgers the way midwestern farm boys are involved with crops and livestock. His uncle was Sakichi, the hardheaded inventor and entrepreneur and the man who insisted that his favorite nephew study engineering at the university—an educational dream he never had for his own son, Kiichiro, Eiji's cousin.

Eiji's mechanical engineering degree, in 1936, came just in time for him to lend a certain contemporary expertise to Kiichiro's new production system, now called "lean manufacturing" or "just-in-time delivery." As we'll see, it would transform Toyota, and eventually the rest of automobile manufacturing around the world. The idea was simple. Unlike Detroit's companies, Toyota and other Japanese carmakers had little or no space to spare for warehousing parts and components. The only way the company could deliver quality automobiles priced the same as or cheaper than Detroit cars was to receive the vendor-produced part *exactly* in time for it to be installed on the unit for which it was intended. Deliver it too early or too late and the profit margin would shrink or disappear.

Eiji's first job at Toyota was running the laboratory in Tokyo, where he convinced a number of young engineers and scientists to come on board. These later became the people who helped Toyota achieve a reputation for technical precision. With the lab up and running, Eiji moved over to the shop floor, where he helped to enhance planning for maintenance and production.

After the devastation of Japan at the end of World War II in the Pacific, Eiji labored day and night to keep the company solvent in the face of runaway inflation and unimaginable destruction (American bombers had destroyed close to half the plant in Toyota City). He cleverly created a new company, Toyota Motor Sales, that kept all financial transactions internal. It worked well for nearly 40 years, until he brought both companies back together.

When he visited the States in 1950, Eiji felt encouraged that he found nothing that was beyond Toyota's capability. The trick was to beat the Americans at their own game—to assemble cars fast in small batches rather than to depend on wasteful and expensive stockpiling. He and his production engineer, Taiichi Ohno, dubbed this the *kanban* system, ordering components just before they fit into a car on the production line.

A further refinement to *kanban* had to do with stopping the line and fixing a problem as it arose. The Americans, he noticed during his tours, kept the line moving no matter what, with the intention of fixing problems at the end of production. All too often, intention was as far as they got. Among Eiji's great innovations was the emphasis on fixing defects as they were discovered—even if it meant stopping the line. He took this even further by empowering each Toyota worker to stop the line. Up until this point, the moving and unstoppable production line had been a linchpin of Detroit's success. The idea at Toyota that a lowly assembly worker could bring the line to a screeching and dramatic halt was light-years ahead of all other automobile manufacturers and led directly to Toyota's dominance in the industry for decades. Eiji always maintained that this idea was not original to him—it belonged to Sakichi and his early work with automatic looms. Back then, stopping the loom upon noticing a defect was even more critical—a defect in weaving would simply pass the error into the entire cloth and render it useless, a waste of time, effort, and money.

On the first day of 1955, Eiji drove Toyota's first production car, the Crown, off the line and into the showroom, where Japanese car buyers, thirsty for anything Japanese after 10 years of reconstruction, bought every car the company could make. Sensing a triumph, Eiji proudly introduced the Crown to American buyers two years later. In American lingo, it turned out to be a lemon. It was not up to the kind of speeds Americans were used to on their flat and endless highways. The shock absorbers were designed for the dreadful potholes in Japan's postwar roads, not the smooth concrete or paved roads in the United States. And the radiator tended to boil over. Eiji watched grimly as Chevys and Fords whizzed by the disabled Crowns as they languished by the roadside, notable for the clouds of steam emanating sadly from the engines.

He learned his lessons. Nearly a decade later, he presented first the Corona and, later, the Corolla (both names suggestive of crowns and royalty—images too good to throw away), and they were instant successes.

In his quiet way, Eiji saw the future. Even better, he test-drove it. He bought a few Mercedes and BMWs and took them apart, wondering if the world was ready for a luxury car made in Japan. The world was. In 1989, Lexus grabbed the attention of elite car buyers and has never let go.

Eiji's last big idea was to set up production facilities in the United States and deliver the cars directly to the market. Once again, his idea, like his production philosophy, was just in time. Japanese cars produced in America primarily by American workers was an idea whose time had come. It was a fitting capstone to Eiji Toyoda's groundbreaking career. Except for one last honor.

Visitors to the Automotive Hall of Fame in Dearborn, Michigan, can enjoy seeing the faces and hearing the words of wisdom of the premier carmakers in the world. Alongside such visionaries as Henry Ford, Walter Chrysler, Alfred Sloan, of General Motors, Edouard Michelin, Ransom Olds, and Harvey Firestone, there is a magnificent portrait of Eiji Toyoda, where he is credited with helping to build the third-largest automobile company in history.

Chapter Three

From Looms to Cars

The story of Toyota automobiles really begins on a day of which no one is certain. It was probably in the year 1887. But it could have been a year or two earlier. Was it winter or spring? Was it time for planting or harvesting? No one knows, for that day has been lost to history. It was surely, however, the taking of that first step that would lead directly to the day the first Toyota Crown automobile came rolling into the sunshine of a new future for Japan. Ironically, it was the first step taken by a man who never designed an automobile himself, nor had he ever dreamed of doing so.

It was the day young Sakichi Toyoda—only 18 or 19—looked at his mother's weaving loom in the corner of his house and thought for the first time that by examining how the loom was made, he could improve its workings. He had seen his mother working on the loom after supper almost every day of his life. But this day was the first day he thought he could apply his imagination and make a better loom that she could use to produce more fabric—and more income—for the Toyoda family.

We may see the young man handling the loom with an air of respect—it was his honorable mother's loom, after all. He hefts its weight and notes how the frame has loosened somewhat with years of working. He recalls how his mother swiftly operates the machine with slender and practiced hands. He sees her operating the shuttle as fast as is humanly possible, and yet still not fast enough to produce real income for the family. No one could operate this particular loom fast enough to make it truly profitable. Profit comes with efficiency, and his mother had maximized the efficiency out of this loom.

He would think about it and try to build a better loom.

Characteristically, the young man never looked to anyone else for help or even advice. He would do it all himself. He studied his mother's loom and the looms of other women in the village. He measured them and built prototypes out of bamboo and other woods that had been tossed as scrap. He built what he thought was a better model, tried it out, and, if it didn't measure up, dismantled it and started over. Working in his spare time, he built and took apart looms for years.

When Sakichi was 23, his world changed.

In that year (1890), Japan held the Third National Industrial Exhibition, in Tokyo. The first exhibition was held in 1877, and others would be held about once every five years thereafter. The site was in Ueno Park, where a steam locomotive chugged through the entire exhibit regularly. The last exhibition was held in Osaka in 1903, when interest in exhibitions and World Fairs began to wane all over the globe. The slogan for the original exhibition was "Enrich the country and strengthen the military; encourage new industry." While that is not exactly a slogan for the ages, the Toyota Motor Corporation would come to fulfill all three of those elements.

Hundreds of the latest machines and production goods from all over the world were on display, to the delight and amazement of the crowds that visited. Sakichi informed his family of his decision to attend and got no encouragement from them. The stout-minded young man didn't need it. He took a train to the big city and walked to the exhibition. It was beyond his wildest dreams—machines as far as the eye could see, chunking and huffing and popping to their own rhythms or placed on pedestals and tables like exquisite pieces of art. He was entranced.

The exhibit ran for four months; Sakichi was there every minute for about two weeks. He stood in line before the doors opened and was the last to leave at night. Like an artist with his sketchpad at the Louvre, he sat on the floor and studied the machines made by Western geniuses and sketched every one on a large paper pad. The looms, especially, were intricate beyond anything he had been able to conceive on his own. He was not discouraged by their complexity—he was inspired.

After the exhibition closed, he stayed in the city and called on every manufacturing company that would let him in. "May I see your looms? May I—if you please—see them operating, and if it is not forbidden, may I make a drawing of them?"

Sakichi was obsessed with the mechanical principles of looms. He would master them, and he would make looms even bigger and more formidable.

The Meiji government was on his side, to a point. In its view, there were pilot projects to be mounted. There were Western factories to be bought and dismantled and shipped over to the island nation and rebuilt in painstaking detail. There were workers to train and a whole new world beyond the samurai and the ancient traditions to be explored.

Take a Free Tour of Toyota's U.S. Plant

Toyota Motor Manufacturing, Kentucky (TMMK), is the largest of the company's manufacturing facilities outside Japan. TMMK provides two-hour tram tours of all 7.5 million square feet of floor space. The 7,000 workers at the plant output nearly 2,000 vehicles a day. That works out to two new vehicles every minute. The welding operations are performed almost exclusively by robots, while human beings assemble all the difficult parts with great care.

You can call the plant in Georgetown, Kentucky, or visit it online at www.toyotageorgetown.com.

Toyota's TMMK Web site links Sakichi's early engineering method with modern Toyota manufacturing:

> Sakichi Toyoda was the inventor of automatic looms who founded the Toyota Group. He invented a loom in 1902 that would stop automatically if any of the threads snapped. His invention opened the way for automated loomworks that allowed a single operator to handle dozens of looms.
>
> Sakichi's invention reduced defects and raised yields, since a loom would not go on producing imperfect fabric and using up thread after a problem occurred. The principle of designing equipment to stop automatically and call attention to problems immediately is crucial to the Toyota Production System. It is evident on every production line at Toyota and at other companies that use the system.

What Sakichi learned about the efficient operation of looms ran counter to the theory of mass production, where the line never stops. Making a loom stop automatically was a breathtaking innovation in its day. Many manufacturers abroad who heard of it were aghast at the audacity of such a thing. In theory, looms would be stopping all the time and profits would disappear. But, in practice, Sakichi was actually discovering that there were economies to be enjoyed by continuously improving production and catching defects immediately at their source.

SAKICHI SEES AN OPPORTUNITY

Sakichi saw his opportunity as bridging the gap between the gigantic, expensive Western looms and the cheap, inefficient Japanese looms. If he could make a reliable machine that served the needs of local weavers, he would find himself alone in the marketplace. It was just where he wanted to be.

He finished his first operational loom several months later, tested it with local weavers, and found it to be a significant advance over anything then in use among small enterprises. He applied for a patent (a practice he would continue dozens of times) and received it from the Meiji government. The young carpenter had disappeared; the young inventor had supplanted him. He would move to Tokyo and begin the first steps toward becoming a wealthy businessman.

EARLY CHALLENGES

The transition was difficult. Even his improved looms depended on human operators. He could not make a profit against those weavers who invested in Western-manufactured looms. He was under constant financial pressure and felt more than ever that he was just a country boy in the big city.

On one of his trips home, he realized just how true that was. His mother had found him a bride, in the country tradition. He had already disappointed his ill and rapidly aging father by rejecting his advice and his occupation, and he had no resolve left to contradict his mother. He got married; from the start he realized it was a mistake but didn't know how to fix it. Ironically, the man whose genius was in finding and fixing mistakes couldn't fix an important one in his own life. He took his new bride back to Tokyo, where he spent every waking hour designing new looms and fixing old ones. He tried hard for three years, but in the end his work proved unable to generate a profit. His business failed. He returned home with an unhappy wife and a heart full of regrets. Perhaps carpentry and the beckoning rice fields were where his future lay, after all.

As often happens, however, family came to his rescue. His uncle had a scheme to get in on the rapid countrywide expansion of railroads by creating a new generation of railroad ties made out of ceramics. Possibly with the good memory of the locomotive running through the National Industrial Exhibition, he leaped at the chance. Part of the attraction for him may have been the opportunity to leave his wife, for whom he evidently had little affection, behind in Yamaguchi.

Whatever the appeal, Sakichi quickly discovered he had no more interest in ceramics than he had in farming. He was a textile man. And so he convinced his uncle to let him raise funds for the ceramics business by inventing an improved yarn-reeling machine. The technology for creating yarn had hardly improved since the old spinning-wheel days celebrated in fairy tales, and Sakichi threw himself into the project.

Once again, he studied a machine in current use, copied it down to the micrometer level, and devised ways to improve it. (Many years later, his son would mimic the process with Fords and Chevrolets.) He ended up designing a machine that, like the sewing machines just coming into use, employed a foot pedal for power and released one hand for speeding up the work of spinning.

He applied for and received a patent, then began selling the machines from factory to factory. Sales were good. He delivered the research funds to his uncle as promised. But ceramics—to no one's surprise but his uncle's—proved unsuitable for the high-impact business of supporting trains.

The only positive aspect of the experience came when his wife delivered his first son, whom they named Kiichiro.

Sakichi, unfortunately, proved no better at being a father than he was a husband. His wife's family, insulted at the way he wasted his hours at the office on research, demanded that she return to her own family. The young boy would stay with Sakichi's parents. The couple divorced.

Feeling freer than he had in a long time, Sakichi partnered with two other men in the city of Nagoya and began selling yarn-reeling machines, working in his spare time on creating a large power loom that would stand against the popular foreign ones.

But fate seemed always to conspire against him.

His business partners proved dishonest and abandoned the store, leaving Sakichi to shoulder the debts. In order to pay them, he had to once again turn his back on his dream of a power loom.

In time, with the debts paid, he hired others to sell machines for him and returned to his laboratory. This time, he brought a new wife with him—a woman who was capable in the store and, best of all, trustworthy.

His notes reveal that just before the turn of the twentieth century, he had a power loom up and running to his great satisfaction. The machine was exponentially more efficient than hand-powered looms, of course, and the finished cloth it produced was of superior quality. The only significant weakness was that it was made mostly of wood and not nearly as durable as its Western metal counterparts.

Sakichi's luck once again ran against him. His machine appeared just in time for an economic recession. He decided to pull inward and wait it out, as his ancestors had done when the divine wind reduced Kublai Khan's fleet to flotsam. During this dormant period, Sakichi turned his skills to designing and making a steel loom that could make cloth sized to international standards.

THE SPIRIT OF *KAIZEN* IS BORN

It was also during this time that he came to realize the overwhelming value of constant improvement. The Japanese term is *kaizen,* and Sakichi made it the cornerstone theory of his professional life. This foundational philosophy of *kaizen* would have permanent influence on all companies that carried the Toyoda name, including the automobile maker that would be called officially Toyota. And it took the U.S. manufacturing community by storm in the 1980s and 1990s.

Western manufacturers traditionally believed that good enough was good enough. Profits lay in getting a good or slightly better product to market as fast as possible and wringing every nickel out of it. They resisted any philosophy that said that no product was ever finished. To be fair, many Western manufacturers had good reason to take pride in their products. Ivory bar soap, for example, has been 99 and 44/100ths percent pure for generations, and no one has yet figured out how to improve it, save for its packaging. Leon Leonwood Bean's Maine Hunting Shoe has scarcely needed an improvement since 1912. Such products as these, however, are relatively simple to make and have few components. A power loom, with its hundreds of constantly moving parts, is a different matter altogether. An automobile, with its thousands of moving parts, is in a different universe altogether. To suggest that the manufacturing of every complex product was subject to continuous improvement was to shift the lines on an ancient playing field. Sakichi Toyoda changed the rules of manufacturing, and they stayed changed.

One byproduct of a belief in *kaizen* is readily apparent: It is expensive. For Sakichi, the expense was borne almost completely by him and his indefatigable labor in the research lab. However, to move up in scale to an automobile is to put your profits at risk every day. The philosophy started by Sakichi on his worktables would be carried to an economically perilous point by his son Kiichiro.

The hand of history continued writing for those Toyoda companies. Sakichi's focus was on research and development, not sales. While his company was doing well, it distracted him from his true work. In 1906, he agreed to a business partnership with Mitsui Trading Company, in which he ceded all his patent rights to them, enabling him to concentrate on his engineering designs. The new firm became Toyoda Loom Works.

Again a recession hit, and Sakichi resigned amid great internal conflict. He lost forever the rights to the machines made with his name stamped on them.

ON TO AMERICA

Depressed, he decided to truly get away from it all. He left his island home for the first time and sailed to America. Upon landing in Seattle in 1910, he boarded a train for a cross-country trip. During the journey, he saw never-imagined sights through his compartment window. In Japan, one could *stroll* across the entire island in a matter of days. The American landscape that unfolded at 10 miles per hour before his eyes dazzled him. It was huge! No wonder the Americans were outdistancing all other manufacturers and inventors. Look at these vistas! He could travel for days and see hardly another human soul or any evidence of civilization. Mountains and prairies stretched out in front of him. At times it seemed as if the journey would go on forever. The trip both exhilarated and saddened him. How could a small isolated island like Japan ever hope to compete with this? There was no end to the wheat fields. Running, clear water was everywhere. Animals roamed the prairies that seemed as vast as the ocean he had just crossed. And everywhere there were towns and cities and villages and an entire robust people with no traditions to lock them into a social stratum and no lack of natural resources on which to build. Everything the Americans put their hands on seemed to grow and prosper and vibrate with energy. It was the New World; seeing it for the first time in his late forties, Sakichi realized he would never have enough time left in his life to be a part of it.

One thing stood out among all the wonders he saw: automobiles. Although Mr. Ford's production cars had become available only two or three years before, it seemed as if every man, woman, and child in the United States was riding in one. There were the famous Ford Model T cars, affectionately called Tin Lizzies, as well as trucks, tractors, motorcycles—all stamped with big American logos and all huffing away at eye-popping speeds. Harvey Firestone, a long-time friend of Henry Ford's, was churning out better and better rubber-composite tires to help drivers navigate the treacherous ruts and gullies that had been gouged out by horse carriages. Sakichi had seen a car or two on the streets of Nagoya the year before, but this was ridiculous. These were not wealthy people, these big smiling farmers driving along the dirt roads wearing floppy hats and thick gloves. These were regular folks, and they were riding like only the truly rich could in Japan!

Sakichi tried hard not to be dismayed, but this was really too much. He called on American loom companies with a heavy heart and soon found his spirits lifted with a joy he hadn't felt since coming to this impossibly big country: His looms were better than theirs. He toured the assembly rooms and machine shops. He asked polite questions in his schoolboy English and took discreet notes. He had failed, despite his bravest efforts, in Japan. But now here he was in the New World, and he felt a decidedly un-Japanese pleasure in feeling that perhaps he could set up shop in this country and beat these loom makers at their own game.

He sought advice from a former countryman now making his home in New York, Dr. Jokichi Takamine, the famous chemist and the man who had discovered the awesome power of human adrenaline. As company historians relate the meeting, Dr. Takamine discouraged Sakichi from emigrating to the States, suggesting that Japan was where his destiny and the needs of his country would meet. The United States could take care of itself; Japan needed his energy and his imagination if it was ever to compete with the rest of the world. It was a hard message, but Sakichi was a patriot of the first order.

Sakichi reluctantly agreed to the good doctor's advice and went home refreshed with a new ambition to bring glory to himself and his country. He would throw himself once more into the textile business and see if he could make things happen there.

SAKICHI'S LUCK CHANGES

Sakichi Toyoda went into debt once again to build his own spinning mill, capitalizing a medium-size operation with several thousand spindles. Once again the divine wind blew, and this time it was favorable to him and to Japan.

World War I had erupted in Europe.

Orders for Toyoda spinning machines flooded in as weavers all over Europe tried desperately to keep up with the demand for cloth to make uniforms, cots, socks, gloves—the whole gamut of war materiel. The company flourished.

By war's end, the renamed Toyoda Spinning & Weaving Company was at full production capacity. But Sakichi had still not realized his dream of an automatic loom that would outperform all others. He turned to the research laboratory with fresh zeal.

By 1924, Sakichi had invented what he called the "Type-G" automatic loom. It was remarkable for several reasons. For one, it featured the first-ever nonstop shuttle that kept moving even when it changed direction. For another, it replenished thread automatically without slowing down—a huge improvement in efficiency that enabled textile companies to greatly improve their profit margins. Because of this machine alone, Japanese weavers were able at last to compete in international markets.

The Type-G was such an advance in technology that five years later Platt Brothers & Co., Ltd., of Great Britain, the industry leader, paid the equivalent of one million yen for the rights to the machine. It was seed money from these exact funds that was used to research and develop the first Toyota motor cars. (Some recent historians claim that the seed money was actually less than half that amount. Whatever the actual figure, virtually all of it went to support Sakichi's son's ambition to make motor cars.)

Sakichi Toyoda, the man who rejected his father's rice-planting farm, had finally found a use for "seed" resources after all. The money and the inspiration for Toyota cars came from Sakichi; the drive and the vision would come from his son Kiichiro. Interestingly, the Toyoda family remains in the textile business to this day.

KIICHIRO TOYODA: THE MAKER AND HIS MACHINES

Shortly after Kiichiro graduated from Tokyo University with a degree in mechanical engineering, in 1920, he turned his inventive skills to improving the machines his father had designed. He was good at it, improving an automatic shuttle device and designing a new mechanism for stopping the loom when the thread broke—some say it was just to prove that he could do it.

But the divine wind whispered again on September 1, 1923. A massive earthquake struck Japan just before noon. Like the infamous San Francisco earthquake a few years earlier, in 1906, the devastation from the quake itself was minor compared to the damage caused by the wildfires that broke out across the region. Transportation and communications all over the nation halted. It would have helped the situation greatly if Japan had trucks and motorized tractors, but there were few. Even the Japanese army was ill prepared, with its small number of heavy vehicles. The government ordered hundreds of truck bodies from Ford in the United States, giving that company a large foothold and an even larger advantage over domestic manufacturers. General Motors came in a year later.

Kiichiro may have started thinking seriously about automobiles during this time. For all his differences with his father, he understood that the old gentleman had built companies whose focus was machinery. It wasn't much of a hook on the young man's imagination, but it was enough. The hook was set deep when Sakichi suggested to his son, the mechanical genius, that the time had come to start thinking about motor cars. Sakichi made the hook permanent when he gave Kiichiro the seed money with the proviso that the young man had to use the funds only for research on building cars. The father had his way at last, and the son was finally obedient in the tradition of old Japan.

Sakichi had developed the loom business by visiting his competitors abroad. Kiichiro would do the same. Even though the challenge of building cars was exponentially more complex than building looms, the *process* of research and development was the same. This respect for process was the foundation of all that was to follow for the automobile company named Toyota.

KIICHIRO'S WORLD TOUR

Notebook in hand, the engineer set off to visit plants in Great Britain and the United States. The managers of those plants must have gotten a chuckle out of seeing the awkward young Asian man with the thick spectacles peering at the mountains of steel parts and clanking assembly lines and masses of gloved workers with their black lunch boxes and grimy faces. One can almost hear the men on the line in their whispered conversations as Kiichiro went by:

"He's not even a car guy."

"Really? What is he?"

"Not sure. They say his daddy builds looms in Japan."

"Looms? For what?"

"Not sure."

"Why is he here?"

"Not sure."

"Hey, you guys, knock it off," says the foreman. "New engine block coming down the line."

They must have noticed the look on his face as he came to comprehend that there was nothing in Japan like this: unlimited, high-quality steel stamped out into fenders and hoods and engine blocks by custom-built machinery spread out over hundreds of acres along places like the Rouge River in Detroit. America was leading the Industrial Age, and, as in everything else America did at the dawn of the twentieth century, it planned to dominate. Some of the plants Kiichiro toured were bigger and more populated than some cities in his country. There was a steam-driven clamor about the landscape that the son of rice farmers could barely comprehend. This was industry on a massive, world-dominating, mind-numbing scale—and it had been going on for decades.

But what the managers thought was awe on the young engineer's face was really a growing sense that *we can do this.* There were instructors right now at Tokyo University who were applying their knowledge of metallurgy and mechanical engineering to the growing industry of motor-powered vehicles. Under the supervision of the Meiji government, Japanese mechanics were taking apart American sedans and British sports cars and identifying and labeling each part and working on specifications so that they could be reproduced by Japanese workers in Japanese factories. Japanese workers themselves were skilled and highly motivated. The winds of change again were blowing across Japan and bringing with them an urgent desire to show the rest of the world what the superior Japanese culture—stiffened by centuries of poverty and strengthened by respectful traditions—could do.

Kiichiro studied Ford's famous moving assembly line. The mechanics of it were simple. It was the *idea* of bringing the growing car to each worker down the line and the *idea* of never stopping the line and the *idea* of one man making one move or assembling one part for his entire work day—often for his entire working life—that entranced Kiichiro. We can do this, he thought. And what's more—we can do it better! No one is sure when the notion of *kaizen* applied to car making first entered Kiichiro's mind, but it could have been on the tour of the River Rouge plant. Ford's scheme was to assemble the units as quickly and as efficiently as possible—without stopping the line!—and to fix any mistakes at the end of the assembly.

What's more, the Ford managers and plant supervisors did not want to hear of problems. Problems meant there were mistakes, and mistakes ate into profits, and Henry Ford was not the man to take loss of profits lightly. If you stopped the line for any reason save a dire emergency, Mr. Ford would hear about it, and it would ruin his day. No supervisor at any Ford plant wished to ruin Mr. Ford's day.

The young engineer with the intense, brooding eyes wrote it all down. He would think about this back in Tokyo. For now, he would take his notes and observe as only a brilliant engineer could. The American carmakers do not want to hear about problems. But are problems not good? Where there is a problem, there is opportunity for improvement. No problems, no improvement. The Americans hated the very idea of a problem on the line; they did everything in their power to avoid problems. Kiichiro thought that this was a weakness. Problems are good. Problems drive solutions, and solutions drive quality.

Kaizen: The Five S Program

Manufacturers throughout the world now employ some form of Toyota-style *kaizen* program to enhance the quality of their products and to motivate workers. One of the more popular programs, called "Five S," employs the *kaizen* philosophy in improving the visual context of one's office or workstation.

1. *Seiri:* Clean up your workspace. It is your work sanctuary.
2. *Seiton:* Sort out the objects you work with; toss them or optimize their location.
3. *Seiso:* Weed out dead projects and old files.
4. *Seiketsu:* Standardize your space so that a substitute could function in it.
5. *Shitsuke:* Keep improving your workspace every day.

On the way home from his world tour, Kiichiro read and studied his prized copy of *My Life and Work* by Henry Ford. He saw it as a training manual on how to build and sell motor cars. It was a manual he was intent on improving—continuously.

FROM LOOMS TO AUTOS

One of his first actions on getting back to Japan was to install a conveyor system at the loom factory. Next he commandeered a corner of the plant and, with an assistant, took apart a small motorcycle engine to study just how different gasoline engines were from looms. He bought machine tools and metal-shaping machines from abroad. In his mind, he was gearing up to go into full-scale automobile production in Japan.

It seemed an insurmountable challenge to all but Kiichiro. By 1930, Ford and General Motors cars were pouring off the assembly lines in Japan, while Japanese cars were still being hand crafted.

Once again, as it was wont to do, the big wide world outside the walls of the loom company was shifting on the tectonic plates of history. China was rattling its sabers in Manchuria, which Japan had acquired during the war with Russia. America and Great Britain were pushing for arms limitations with Japan. The times were calling for trucks. Japan's generals needed trucks to carry soldiers and the heavy weapons of war into the north, where Russia and China loomed as formidable adversaries.

Kiichiro, as far as anyone can tell, paid little attention to the headlines; his mind was engaged in the myriad details of micrometers and the surface tension of different motor oils. By 1933, he was done with motorcycle engines and ready to move up to passenger cars. For that he needed significant capital. And the key to the cash profits of the recently renamed Toyoda Automatic Loom Works was held by his older stepbrother, Risaburo. "How much more do you need?" Risaburo asked. "Beside the one million yen our father left you in his will?" "Oh, one or two more million," Kiichiro responded. It was the equivalent of asking for 20 to 40 million U.S. dollars today.

This was a delicate moment for Risaburo. He was the eldest son, of course, but his name was not *really* Toyoda. The real scion of the Toyoda family was now in front of him, his hand held out for money in what any observer might take as a rude gesture. Kiichiro needed the money, and Risaburo had it.

Maybe, Risaburo said. Kiichiro took that as a yes and began hiring experts.

He also bought cars.

He brought a new Chevrolet into his corner of the loom factory and took it apart piece by piece, just as he had the motorcycle engine. His engineers made scale drawings of each part as it was laid onto the floor, like the skeleton of a dinosaur brought in from a dig. Piece by piece and part by part, Kiichiro soon had complete plans and drawings of everything that went into an American car. Now the tricky part: to find a way to duplicate each piece, assemble the pieces, and put the Toyoda name on it. It was a trick that would take years to master. In the meantime, in the absence of any decent sheet-metal-making capacity in Japan, he decided to build his own steel mill.

Steel for Swords, Not Cars

Japan had long had access to good-quality iron, and its craftsmen had long ago learned how to make nearly pure quality carbon. For centuries, Japanese craftsmen had known how to combine iron and carbon and other exotic ingredients and to apply intense heat to make a kind of steel that the world had never seen before.

The ingredients and the process, however, were considered sacred, and limited, for this was the steel that went into making swords for samurai warriors. Artisans knew how to separate brittle compound from malleable compound and knew how to form the hard steel around a soft steel core to make swords of astonishing strength with an edge that no other steel-shapers had been able to match.

What Japanese craftsmen did not know how to do was to stamp out industrial-grade steel in vast quantities.

It didn't take Kiichiro Toyoda long to find out.

The additional two or three million yen ran through Kiichiro's fingers like water, and he looked around for more.

He made an impassioned plea to the board of directors of the loom company, and they agreed to another two million yen. They even changed the articles of incorporation to reflect the company's new interest in automobiles. Kiichiro had bought more time.

Then he sent two engineers overseas to buy the tools and technologies for making automobile parts. Buying the products was one thing; learning how to put them together and use them was another. They had to learn the intricacies of metal, glass, paint, leather, insulation, oil, and rubber. They had to learn how to take the machines apart for maintenance and how to put them back together; how to mold sheet metal for a wide range of applications; how to apply chrome and paint to metal for an aesthetically pleasing look. And they had to learn how to do all this in a matter of months, all the while studying ways to do the work faster and cheaper so that Kiichiro could keep the prices down for Japanese consumers, who were eternally strapped for cash.

AN IDEA JUST IN TIME

Back home, Kiichiro was pondering how to modify the American style of stockpiling and wasting what was left over to fit his situation of greatly reduced resources and far less space in which to work. He could stockpile little and waste nothing. To waste time or material was unthinkable. His profit margins would be so small as to be hardly noticeable for years. The slightest waste would toss his fledgling enterprise into financial ruin and kill his idea of a Japanese car for Japanese people before it even got onto the road. Americans could afford waste of almost any magnitude; he could afford none at all.

It was a problem he would solve or else face utter failure and loss of face. Perhaps even worse, failure would drag down with it the magnificent loom and spinning companies his father had built with sheer willpower alone. The ramifications of failure were so great that Kiichiro could not bear to think of them for more than a few minutes at a time. He turned his concentration to making automobiles in a uniquely Japanese way—a way he would have to create out of his own imagination and limited experience. Few entrepreneurs and inventors have had to face the possibility of such catastrophic failure. Kiichiro Toyoda knew that he must succeed or else destroy the lives of his extended family and the hundreds of workers who depended on the Toyoda name for their livelihood.

With the technologies and machines coming together at last, he began to think of a way to bring them all together with life-or-death efficiency. His solution—often called "just-in-time manufacturing" or "lean production"—would change the way industries made products across the globe well into the twenty-first century.

MEANWHILE, BACK IN THE SHOP . . .

In September 1934, Kiichiro had his first engine. He called it the Type A. It was a 3,389-cc power plant with a full six cylinders blasting away. When the Type A first burbled into action, thundering its noise across the shop floor, workers came from all over ready to cheer the boss's success. But Kiichiro, being a Toyoda and not given to sentiment of any kind, said he would celebrate when they tested the output to see how it measured up to Detroit's finest. It didn't. At 30 horses, it had half the power of the Chevrolet engine on which it was based. He sent the engine people back to the lab to discover where it was losing power.

There were other challenges.

The crew had so far stamped out the sheet-metal body by hand. Production would require sheet-metal presses, and no one in the country had yet figured out how to make dies that would resist crushing under tremendous pressure. The nation was far behind even Europe in being able to make and process the materials such as glass windscreens and chrome trim and leather seating that made any automobile attractive to buyers. And looming directly over Kiichiro's head was his own Damoclesian sword of cost. How on earth could he hope to keep costs below what the American carmakers paid in their own country? Ford and Chevrolet could make cars in Japan using parts and accessories shipped in from the United States and still sell at prices lower than Toyoda's best efforts—featuring higher quality and better workmanship.

LET IT BE TRUCKS

Frustrated beyond his ability to speak of it, Kiichiro decided to increase his chances of being profitable by producing trucks as well as cars. It is testament to his willpower that he determined that it would not be an either/or situation. Where most leaders would have chosen one over the other, he decided to do both. A lesser man would have apologized to everyone and gone back to making automatic looms.

Kiichiro was committed—to his family, to the memory of his father, to his employees, to his government, to his own faith in himself. He would do this. He would make cars or die. First, however, he would make trucks. More than that—he would start making trucks in as little as a year.

The market for Japanese trucks was wide open, given the increasing demand of the army for vehicles that would hold up under daunting conditions such as driving on primitive roads, carrying heavy ordnance, and operating in a range of weather from frozen tundra to sun-baked sand.

Army generals were less demanding than civilian car buyers, anyway. The trucks could come in a variety of configurations, with little concern for aesthetics. Further, the Imperial Army was intimately familiar with the usual shortages in Japan, so it was happy to accept trucks that were made simply and cheaply. If the truck had only one headlight, so be it, as long as the thing carried water barrels and .50-caliber machine guns to the front lines.

The engine that he had copied from Chevrolet would do for trucks as well as sedans. The Ford-designed steering and drive trains would adapt easily to trucks. The DeSoto body looked perfectly in place on a canvas-covered pickup. Everything, in fact, was ready, including the miniature production plant and the fledgling steel mill. If a cynic once in a while suggested that the Toyoda car facility was also free of the burden of cash, no one noticed. Some form of motorized vehicle would come flowing out of that plant soon, and Kiichiro would drive the first one out.

Company records show that the first "Model A1" passenger car made its appearance in May 1935. It looked like a Western car because it was styled after several of them. It boasted a showy art deco chrome grille and the slicked-back profile of a short limousine. Whatever its shortcomings, it was a car and it was made in Japan. There would be no turning back. Employees erected a tent and had a Shinto priest perform a short ceremony. Kiichiro watched the proceedings solemnly; he thought of how his father would have loved to be here at this moment.

There was little time for emotion. Now that several prototypes of the A1 were bouncing along the rough roads in Japan, it was time to turn everyone's full attention to trucks.

MANAGERS LEARN TO SWEAT

Sometime during this period, Kiichiro established a kind of semiformal policy he had learned from his father—a policy that all Toyota managers would practice from then on. The fledgling car company would practice a "hands-on" style. The principle is simple: Few things are to be learned in one's office. Managers roll up their sleeves and get to work out where the real work is. One finds and corrects problems by seeing them up close with one's own eyes. Theory is fine for the classroom at the university; successful businesspeople get their hands dirty. Two generations later, when Toyota was banging heads with Detroit's leading carmakers for worldwide supremacy, this policy came into stark relief.

Detroit executives sailed to work in chauffeur-driven limousines. They bypassed the noisy factory floor to catch elevators that whisked them up to skyscraper offices where people spoke in whispers and there was not even the hint of the smell of motor oil. They frequently left early for lunch and just as frequently talked business with each other between putts at the country club.

Toyota executives, in contrast, walked the factory floor every day and surprised no one when they dropped onto their backs and pushed under a car on the line with a flashlight to search for the source of an annoying rattle caused by a loose screw. They enjoyed few rounds of golf. And lunch was routinely a tuna sandwich eaten while hunched over schematic drawings.

Kiichiro Toyoda, the prototype Toyota manager, rolled up his sleeves and got oil under his fingernails every day. He never learned how to play golf.

The Meiji government was hard at work, as well. As Commodore Perry had learned so long ago, opening up Japan to world trade was no easy task. Keeping it open proved even harder for the big American carmakers.

In 1934, Ford attempted to buy a large piece of land for a bigger factory in Yokohama but was forestalled by the Imperial Army. Tensions between Japan and the United States were building over oil consumption, and America was threatening to get even tougher. The army was concerned that a huge American enterprise so close to Tokyo would impact the solidifying attitudes of both sides. Ford backed down.

A year later, Ford tried again, this time successfully. Japanese workers needed work, regardless of who owned the company. Into the conflict stepped the government, which declared that producing motor vehicles was crucial to national defense. A new law specified that licenses were required for any manufacturer that made more than 3,000 cars a year and that the majority ownership of any such company had to be Japanese.

Kiichiro paid hardly any attention to the new law, as he was working seven days a week trying to build trucks.

The "G1" truck rolled out in August 1935. It was awkward and boxy, far from beautiful. But it worked. It looked like the marriage of a big car and a small truck and could carry nearly two tons. It was sturdy and high off the road, and it would do the job. The cab was tall and roomy. Two headlights gleamed on either side of a tall, ornate grille. The rear half was a box made of wood slats to carry payloads. It looked exactly like a workingman's truck. At its debut in Tokyo, in November, everyone from bureaucrats to generals to farmers was praising it. Maybe best of all, it was just slightly cheaper than its American counterparts. Soon afterwards, however, the defects started showing up.

The trucks broke down in a puff of steam about every 500 miles.

The rear axles seemed about as strong as matchsticks and broke in half with dismaying frequency.

Parts fell off. Doors failed to close tightly. Fuel lines clogged with any change in the weather.

Kiichiro and his engineers hunkered down and worked through all the defects one by one, making repairs for free, sometimes replacing entire vehicles at no charge. Thanks to the power of Kiichiro's *kaizen* philosophy, the defects and mistakes began clearing up, and the company moved into a bigger production plant. Kiichiro worked quietly on plans to speed up and expand production figures.

He also turned back to making cars.

PHAETON = GLAMOUR

The time was right for a little glamour. The A1 was fine for a proto-type, but Detroit was proving that a sleeker look attracted buyers. So he designed the AA with classier lines and a convertible version, the AB Phaeton (FEE-tahn), for some real style.

The biggest challenge now, Kiichiro believed, was to catch up to the West's technical expertise. He needed a research and development man, and he found one in his bright young cousin Eiji (EH-gee) Toyoda, fresh out of engineering school.

Now Kiichiro became a man on fire. He had much catching up to do and little time to do it. He hired the finest engineers and designers he could find. He bought Western engines of all kinds and shipped them to the factory for the by-now standard practice of dissecting them down to the micro-level to see what made them work. He invested in a state-of-the-art research laboratory. He spent money on the things that mattered and paid himself little. He invested in hard work and cared nothing for the trappings of success. He did, in short, all the things for which Toyota Motor Company is now rightly famous.

In an effort to gain national attention, the company announced a con-test open to all Japanese citizens to design a logo for the vehicles and for the new car-making enterprise. It received 27,000 entries. The winner dis-played the Toyoda name written horizontally and enclosed by a circle.

SAYONARA, TOYODA

At that point Fate, wearing a familiar face, stepped in. Risaburo, Ki-ichiro's elder stepbrother, the president of the parent company and a man who never advised Kiichiro on anything, suggested one small change that might help distinguish the car-making company from the loom-making company. How about changing the name slightly to Toyota? One could write *Toyota* with only 8 strokes, rather than the 10 needed for *Toyoda*. Eight was a lucky number in Japan; 10 was not.

Kiichiro accepted the suggestion instantly, and there you have it. He had spent more time deciding what to have for breakfast that morning than in deciding on a name change for the company.

While displaying his new cars and trucks at an exhibit in Tokyo in September 1936, he received official government notice that Toyoda Auto-matic Loom Works had been awarded one of only two licenses to manu-facture automobiles in Japan. The other license went to an obscure, older carmaker called Nissan.

There was celebration at the Toyoda Automatic Loom Works. The fu-ture looked bright indeed. Given enough time, Kiichiro knew he could start turning a profit. After that, he could see a smooth road ahead for the new Toyota brand. The key was time. He was starting from far behind in the race, and the other competitors had technical superiority on their side. But he and his people worked harder, thought harder about constant improvement, and were driven by personal and national pride. Time, he thought—time was all he needed to make it happen. But even he had no idea how little time was left for him and for his beloved country.

In just five years, the Japanese Imperial Navy would drop bombs on American ships at Pearl Harbor, Hawaii, and the divine wind that had blasted apart the armada of Kublai Khan would turn with unimagined ferocity on the Emperor and his people.

THE PROBLEM WITH "MADE IN JAPAN"

Modern marketing theory asserts that the first images associated with any product become permanent in the minds of consumers. This assumption underscores why most producers of products and services are extremely careful about the initial perceptions for their brand. That perception, whatever it is, is likely to last for generations.

Volvo, for example, early on started selling its cars as "safe" alternatives for the motoring public. As seriously as Volvo may try these days to convince people that its cars are stylish, even sexy, it cannot retreat from its central image as a company that makes cars built to keep people safe while inside.

After going head-to-head with Ford for years, Chevrolet decided that it was the middle choice of car for middle-class Americans. Its advertising slogan from the 1940s and 1950s, "See the USA in your Chevrolet," struck exactly the right tone for the time. Postwar Americans, with new cash in their pockets, were in the mood to hit the road and see the sights. Live by it, die by it, however. Whenever Chevy tried to move up in class, that early image fought against the effort. Chevrolet is still a middle choice for middle-class people.

In the beginning, a Toyota was a car that could be depended upon to break down. It became the butt of jokes. Kiichiro and his team worked feverishly to fix defects as they showed up, but sadly they tended to show up on the road—or, rather, by the side of the road. Western-built cars were far ahead. They had financial power and images of high quality behind them. They were American-made, or British-made, in a time when those classifications meant something.

Now the stamp that said "Made in Japan" had about it an implication of poor quality and flimsy materials. This was hardly surprising. After all, only 83 years earlier Commodore Perry had firmly pried open Japan's door to admit Western goods. Kiichiro's father, Sakichi, was born just 14 years after that. And now, one generation later, Kiichiro was trying to compete with carmakers that had been building automobiles and amassing profits and creating technical innovations for more than a quarter of a century. No other modern corporation that is now an industry leader has started from so far behind.

Kiichiro knew he could make the new brand work. He had done the math. In America, every four people enjoyed the services of one automobile. In Japan, if progress kept to its schedule, that figure would be 1 in 10. There were close to 100 million Japanese people. So the marketplace averaged out to about 10 million potential customers. That was huge!

He also knew that he could improve quality and the poor image of Toyota quickly if only he had proper space in which to build vehicles and proper assembly personnel to put them together according to his exacting standards. That would require a far larger factory than the one now stepping on the toes of the loom makers. And it would require a massive investment of capital for newer, larger, more technologically advanced equipment along with the money necessary to train the local peasants in motor car production. Kiichiro could see the path to success clearly, and not that far down the road.

The only fly in the ointment was that, so far, the new brand had yet to turn over so much as one yen in profit. It existed on the back of the loom works profits. Kiichiro had an answer even for this. The trick, he said, was to cut costs. To reduce the quality of the materials any further would be to risk suicide. Therefore, the task was to cut costs by eliminating waste. It was the only answer. And he was just the man to come up with new ways to get rid of waste. It would take an accounting pencil as sharp as a samurai sword and managers as ruthless as Mongol warriors, but it could be done.

Risaburo and the other members of the board of directors believed him. Even more, they felt they had no choice. This was Sakichi's own natural son, and Sakichi had already declared that cars were the future so far as his company was concerned. To this point, Kiichiro had been bleeding the loom company dry of its profits, but that would turn around soon. All it would take would be lots more hard work, some quiet, peaceful years, and a smile from the gods once in a while.

In the meantime, he insisted on yet more working capital and a new factory. The gods must have been smiling somewhere, because the board approved all of it. They even approved the creation of an entirely new company, separate and distinct from the loom works.

Company records show that in August 1937, seven years after the death of Sakichi Toyoda, the Toyota Motor Company, Ltd., declared itself officially open for business.

- Capitalization: 12 million yen
- Line of credit: 25 million yen
- Shares of stock: 240,000 (all owned by family members and associates of the company; virtually no outsiders held a financial interest)

- President: Risaburo Toyoda
- Executive Vice President: Kiichiro Toyoda

Rules for Success, from Father to Son

In 1934, Kiichiro posted on the factory wall for everyone to see a poster containing the business advice he had received from his father, Sakichi Toyoda. It was in formal Japanese, which is why the English translation sounds somewhat stiff.

1. Be contributive to the development and welfare of the country by working together, regardless of position, in faithfully fulfilling your duties.
2. Be ahead of the times through endless creativity, inquisitiveness, and pursuit of improvement.
3. Be practical and avoid frivolity.
4. Be kind and generous; strive to create a warm, homelike atmosphere.
5. Be reverent, and show gratitude for things great and small in thought and deed.

In our twenty-first century, many business leaders, psychologists, authors, and inspirational speakers underscore the vast power of gratitude in one's life. In this area, as in many others, Sakichi Toyoda was a visionary and far ahead of his time

---

Ill blows the wind that profits nobody.

—Shakespeare, *Henry VI,* Part 3

Just a few weeks before the official creation of the Toyota Motor Company, China and Japan had declared war on each other. The timing could not have been worse for world leaders or better for the new car-making company. Orders poured in. The army needed thousands of trucks immediately. This was a boon, for the new company could now make serious profits and work for a patriotic cause.

Kiichiro found a location for the new factory quickly. It was in Koromo, near Nagoya. The site had so many defects as to make many people raise an eyebrow in wonder. It was remote, far from ships or trains, so receiving raw materials and shipping finished products would be complicated.

Kiichiro, far-thinking as always, had a grander vision in mind than merely transportation of goods and products. Recalling his travels in America, especially in his touring of "company towns" such as Detroit and Flint, he could see the value of a town dominated by one organization, a central location in which people could live, work, shop, raise a family, and grow old. What's more, this was a car company, after all. It made cars!

In the new industrial world, thought Kiichiro, our employees can drive to work and drive home. They can even live farther away than bicycles and horse carts would allow. In agricultural Japan, this was new—even shocking—thinking altogether.

But it was exactly the kind of thinking that great inventors are famous for. Thomas Edison envisioned a country where all the citizens could sit on easy chairs and read books by incandescent light, while listening to music selected by themselves and played on a machine that rotated a wax disk. Guglielmo Marconi envisioned a world where ships could send wireless signals to shore-based stations across an ocean and receive news as it happened. The Wright Brothers saw the real possibility that people would one day travel across unthinkable distances inside an airplane. In the same way, Kiichiro Toyoda envisioned every citizen of a newly industrialized Japan floating to work in a gas-powered automobile—a Toyota automobile.

To reach that enchanting future, he would have to invent ways to manufacture an automobile that no one had yet thought of—ways that were simple, repeatable, cost-effective, fast, and profitable. And, while he was at it, why not throw in ways that affirmed the humanity of the workers and brought glory to Japan? He could see it unfolding into the future. To make it happen, he needed time and money. He believed that with enough money he could buy enough time to make everything work. No one could have foreseen, however, that he was already out of time.

He began with money. Since he had so little of it, he would have to invent ways to save it during manufacturing. The Americans and the British could outspend him; they could never outthink him. He turned his sharp mind to the problem of saving while not wasting. If he could shave one yen a week off the cost of production, it would be a start. One hundred yen a week—a world-changing victory. One thousand yen a week— a miracle. As his father had taught him, he was in the miracle business.

A MULTIMILLION-YEN IDEA: JUST IN TIME

Reducing waste could almost be thought of as a Japanese concept. The Japanese were all used to making do with woefully inadequate resources. No other major country was so lacking in natural materials. Few other peoples had subsisted for so long on near-starvation diets. Without the staples of fish and rice, the nation would have withered up and blown away long ago.

Among people so inured to doing without, cutting waste was an obvious place to start. Kiichiro made it his life's work. He walked the plant floor many times a day, observing, taking notes, asking questions. "Why do you keep this tool on that bench? Why not closer?" "How long do you have to wait for a particular part to arrive?" "Where can we position this bolt so you can tighten it faster?" "Why is there a pile of unused components in that corner?"

In their important book on the history of the Toyota Corporation, *Against All Odds*, Yukiyasu Togo and William Wartman describe the challenges he faced:

> With the number of steps involved in the construction of an automobile, a few seconds of waste in each procedure resulted in tremendous cumulative inefficiency—waste that was easy to overlook because it occurred in such small increments....When the variations in work speed were great enough, bottlenecks were created and components piled up in certain areas.

The piling up of components was no big deal in America—the Big Three auto companies built mountains of the stuff anywhere they pleased. Kiichiro had seen them with his own eyes and understood them to be what they really were: mountains of money that eventually blew away and were lost forever. At the time, Ford and GM didn't even think about those piles as a waste of money and resources (they do now!), because profits were coming in and there was work for everybody—an endless demand across the wide American landscape.

Kiichiro was under no such delusions. Five components in a corner meant he was losing money and wasting time. Ten components in each of 10 corners meant he would be out of business in a year. So he applied his brilliant brain to making the company ruthlessly efficient.

True scientific and technical breakthroughs often happen quietly, sometimes unnoticed altogether. Alexander Graham Bell used the device he named a telephone to ask his assistant Watson, in another room, to come and help him with something and was astonished when Watson showed up. No one else in the room thought it was remarkable. Galileo observed the moons of Jupiter through his crude telescope and developed what turned out to be the precise formula for determining the tides on earth; no one noticed for years. Dr. Alexander Fleming, a field surgeon in World War I, discovered the germ-killing power of a bread mold he called penicillin and was ignored for a decade. A world-changing event seldom happens against the background of fireworks.

One fine day in the Toyota shop, Kiichiro walked over to a wall and tacked up a sign that read "Just in time." Years later the concept, deceptively simple as it was, would revolutionize manufacturing across the globe; today, however, was just another day at work. Kiichiro was always putting up motivational signs and slogans, and here was another one.

"Just in time."

When anyone asked him what that meant, he elaborated. He had been thinking about stockpiling and warehousing for many months. He believed that to conquer the problem of waste—all waste, from time to materials to people—would enable him to build a reliable and inexpensive car for the people of Japan.

"Just in time" was at its heart a mechanical principle. Let's say Worker A's job is to attach three bolts and three nuts onto the left rear wheel assembly as the car moves into his station. He could work the way the Americans did, with a bucket of bolts and a bucket of nuts at his feet. However, those nuts and bolts were likely ordered months ago and paid for. They have been on the shop floor for two weeks as the piles in the buckets get smaller and the assemblyman works around them. The money to pay for those components has been spent weeks ago, but the maker will see no return on that money for many more weeks, possibly months or years. Who pays for the use of that money, which could have been gathering interest but hasn't? The money has in effect been sitting in buckets on the shop floor. On an individual scale, this is not much of a loss; on a planetary scale, the loss is formidable. The loss is that much greater if the market slows down and people stop buying cars for a period of time. Now those installed bolts and those installed nuts are becoming dangerously expensive.

Kiichiro's way (soon to be known as the Toyota Production System, or TPS) is to have no buckets. In fact, nothing happens until someone orders a car. If Worker A is operating according to just-in-time principles, he turns and puts his hand out and someone or something gives him three nuts and three bolts, he installs them, and the already ordered car moves on down the line. If one multiplies that effect for hundreds of thousands of times for each car, the result is obvious. Less waste means more profit. It means that capital stays in play, and the power of that capital to earn profit is almost never slowed down.

The ramifications of this system are obvious and complex.

Q: What has to happen for those nuts and bolts to reach Worker A in time?
A: Worker B has to notify the Acme Nuts & Bolts Company and give them 15 minutes to make them and deliver them just in time.
Q: Who alerts Worker B?
A: Good question.

The answer to all such questions resides in a set of manuals known as standard work procedures. It was into the task of envisioning, testing, and codifying such procedures that Kiichiro threw himself. In his spare time, he designed the new manufacturing plant along the lines that his manuals dictated. The plant had to operate according to a brutal logic; there would be no time to reconfigure it, and so there would be no time for mistakes. Mistakes were a waste with the potential to destroy the company.

With the Koromo plant up and running by the end of 1938, Kiichiro was selling trucks to the army as fast as he could produce them. Red ink turned to black. The bitter image of sad little Toyota cars broken down by the roadside morphed into tough military trucks driving into the heart of China. Now family and board members were not the only ones clamoring to buy stock; some big names in the international investment community demanded their own shares as the price climbed higher.

This good news was offset in Kiichiro's mind by a particular piece of bad news. During its first few years in the automobile business Toyota had sold only 1,500 cars. At this point the company was no longer in the car business; it was in the truck business.

The winds changed again. With the China war seemingly without end, American components and raw products slowed to a trickle. Gas and steel became military assets to be apportioned as the generals saw fit. The sight of military uniforms in the plant was not uncommon. Suggestions turned into demands. Japan was rapidly becoming militarized. It had set up army and navy academies after the First World War modeled on the British style, for Great Britain was still a global empire and America had not yet mobilized for its own war to come. Kiichiro found many of his business decisions second-guessed not by stockholders but by military officers and government bureaucrats. At the end of 1939, American carmakers, sensing the storm to come, pulled out of Japan, leaving their Japanese workers to fend for themselves. Some of those workers went to Toyota.

Kiichiro spent the next two years scrounging for scraps of steel and gallons of gasoline and fabric for seat covers. His beloved car company was now a truck company under the near-total control of the military. Western countries that had once demanded that Japan open its doors now withdrew their trade altogether and shut their own doors. Ambassadors talked and political bodies deliberated, but no one could find solutions.

At the end of that second year, on December 7, Japan declared war with the United States of America.

Kiichiro's hopes for a bright future and his meticulous plans for more factories were in shambles. "Just in time" was an idea that was no longer practicable. He would get parts and components—if at all—when the military determined that he could.

Kiichiro once again turned inward, to the satisfaction he always found in research and engineering design. He would stop relying on outside vendors and begin designing and making his own components. He built production machines and created his own tools. He learned more and more about how to make cars from beginning to end, out of necessity emulating Henry Ford and other American carmakers who believed that there were greater profits to be made in supplying all components for a vehicle, including mining the ore and smelting the steel themselves. In time, all carmakers would abandon this costly and cumbersome strategy.

Meanwhile, the war against America and its allies began to drain the blood—literally and figuratively—from Japan. In the beginning, there had been hope and renewed patriotic fervor. When the American Pacific

Fleet was nearly destroyed in Hawaii, the imperial government hoped for a quick peace treaty and restoration of trade. Surely the West would see that Japan had no choice and would understand that a first strike was necessary, given the inequities in size and power between the two nations! But all Japan had done, as one admiral said presciently, was to awaken a sleeping giant. America, with its attention now completely engaged in the Pacific theater, went to full war mode at home. Within a year of Pearl Harbor, the United States was churning out a destroyer a week, a cruiser every 10 days, an aircraft carrier a month, a fighter plane every two hours. Battleships had been pulled out of mothballs and were now filling their 16-inch guns with fresh powder, ready to send a payload the size of a New York taxicab over two miles of open ocean.

There would be no turning back, and no easy peace. One important factor now being studied by historians was the almost total lack of understanding on both sides. The Americans saw the Japanese as egotistical without reason, physically weak, and given to ceremony over substance. The Japanese saw the Americans as lazy and cowardly, the opposite of samurais, people who resisted sacrificing themselves and cared nothing for personal honor.

Both sides were fatally wrong. But the prejudices of both sides contained some kernels of truth. The Americans did prefer life over death; they would surrender when further fighting was pointless. On the other side, for example, Imperial admirals believed in innate Japanese superiority so fervently that they discounted the Americans' growing dependence on the use of radar at sea, believing that Japanese eyes could see farther.

Japan, the island of seafarers, turned its full industrial capacity to making elegant battleships and cruisers in preparation for one great sea engagement in which it would destroy the rest of the American fleet. That one battle never happened; there were several, with names like Coral Sea, Midway, and Leyte Gulf. Japan won some and lost some, but the effort, while valiant, was hopeless. When the Japanese navy lost a ship, it was not replaced. When the Americans lost a ship, two more took its place the next day, five more in a week. It was a war of attrition that Japan did not have the resources to win.

At home, the people descended into privation. Food was rationed for civilians so that soldiers and sailors could eat enough to sustain the fighting. (The definition of "enough" at war's end had boiled down to one small bowl of rice a day.) The people wondered how long they could hold out and never thought of surrendering. The government began amassing forces on the southern edge of the island to repel the invaders who would come as inexorably as the Mongols several centuries before.

In the last year of the war, in May, American firebombs destroyed Kiichiro's house; he moved his family to the suburbs. Germany had surrendered just a few days before, and the war in Europe was over. The Allies now turned the full might of their armies and navies toward the small island nation of Japan.

For the rest of the summer, American planes firebombed more than 60 cities. Suffering, homelessness, and famine had become universal. And still the people held on. It was commonly thought that when the end came, as it must, and enemy soldiers waded ashore the way Kublai Khan's raiders had done, there would be no divine wind to save the Japanese this time. The women and children who were left would fight with sharpened broomsticks if necessary.

Near the end, firebombs found the Koromo factory and nearly destroyed it—years of Kiichiro's labor gone in a flash. On August 6, the B-29 *Enola Gay* dropped an atomic bomb on Hiroshima, effectively leveling the city and destroying all life for several miles. Three days later, to the south and west, another atomic bomb leveled the industrial seaport city of Nagasaki. The Emperor and the people of Japan surrendered. The loss of life was indescribable.

Vast swaths of Japanese civilization and culture had been obliterated. Historians tend to agree that no nation has ever suffered such total devastation as Japan at the end of World War II. Its enemies had finally understood that it would keep fighting until there was little left, and so they made sure to leave little.

The next time the Americans set foot on the island, it was to help the people start rebuilding.

Several important factors contributed to the rapid reconstruction of Japan:

- Although much of the infrastructure had been destroyed, from railroads to power plants to bridges and streets, the cultural and institutional skeleton was still there. In other words, there was something to build on, after all, and it was contained mostly in the lives and spirit of the people.
- The Allied powers worked inside the political structure and gave a Japanese face to most reforms.
- The Meiji government had already experimented with some forms of democracy—rare for any imperial government. At war's end, the people were ready to institute their own kind of democracy and got solidly behind every effort to build it.

RECONSTRUCTION AND THE UNITED STATES

The U.S. State Department (http://www.state.gov/r/pa/ho/time/cwr/91194.htm) provides a vital synopsis of this period in Japan's history:

Occupation and Reconstruction of Japan, 1945–52

After the defeat of Japan in World War II, the United States led the Allies in the occupation and rehabilitation of the Japanese state.

Between 1945 and 1952, the U.S. occupying forces, led by General Douglas A. MacArthur, enacted widespread military, political, economic, and social reforms.

The groundwork for the Allied occupation of a defeated Japan was laid during the war. In a series of wartime conferences, the leaders of the Allied powers of Great Britain, the Soviet Union, the Republic of China, and the United States discussed how to disarm Japan, deal with its colonies (especially Korea and Taiwan), stabilize the Japanese economy, and prevent the remilitarization of the state in the future. In the Potsdam Declaration, they called for Japan's unconditional surrender; by August of 1945, that objective had been achieved.

In September 1945, General MacArthur took charge of the Supreme Command of Allied Powers (SCAP) and began the work of rebuilding Japan. Although Great Britain, the Soviet Union, and the Republic of China had an advisory role as part of an "Allied Council," MacArthur had the final authority to make all decisions. The occupation of Japan can be divided into three phases: the initial effort to punish and reform Japan, the work to revive the Japanese economy, and the conclusion of a formal peace treaty and alliance.

The first phase, roughly from the end of the war in 1945 through 1947, involved the most fundamental changes for the Japanese Government and society. The Allies punished Japan for its past militarism and expansion by convening war crimes trials in Tokyo. At the same time, SCAP dismantled the Japanese army and banned former military officers from taking roles of political leadership in the new government. In the economic field, SCAP introduced land reform, designed to benefit the majority tenant farmers and reduce the power of rich landowners, many of whom had advocated for war and supported Japanese expansionism in the 1930s. MacArthur also tried to break up the large Japanese business conglomerates, or zaibatsu, as part of the effort to transform the economy into a free market capitalist system. In 1947, Allied advisors essentially dictated a new constitution to Japan's leaders. Some of the most profound changes in the document included downgrading the emperor's status to that of a figurehead without political control and placing more power in the parliamentary system, promoting greater rights and privileges for women, and renouncing the right to wage war, which involved eliminating all non-defensive armed forces.

By late 1947 and early 1948, the emergence of an economic crisis in Japan alongside concerns about the spread of communism sparked a reconsideration of occupation policies. This period

is sometimes called the "reverse course." In this stage of the occupation, which lasted until 1950, the economic rehabilitation of
Japan took center stage. SCAP became concerned that a weak
Japanese economy would increase the influence of the domestic
communist movement, and with a communist victory in China's
civil war increasingly likely, the future of East Asia appeared to be
at stake. Occupation policies to address the weakening economy
ranged from tax reforms to measures aimed at controlling inflation. However the most serious problem was the shortage of raw
materials required to feed Japanese industries and markets for
finished goods. The outbreak of the Korean War in 1950 provided
SCAP with just the opportunity it needed to address this problem,
prompting some occupation officials to suggest that, "Korea came
along and saved us." After the UN entered the Korean War, Japan
became the principal supply depot for UN forces. The conflict
also placed Japan firmly within the confines of the U.S. defense
perimeter in Asia, assuring the Japanese leadership that whatever
the state of its military, no real threat would be made against Japanese soil.

In the third phase of the occupation, beginning in 1950, SCAP
deemed the political and economic future of Japan firmly established and set about securing a formal peace treaty to end both
the war and the occupation. The U.S. perception of international
threats had changed so profoundly in the years between 1945
and 1950 that the idea of a re-armed and militant Japan no longer
alarmed U.S. officials; instead, the real threat appeared to be the
creep of communism, particularly in Asia. The final agreement
allowed the United States to maintain its bases in Okinawa and
elsewhere in Japan, and the U.S. Government promised Japan a
bilateral security pact. In September of 1951, fifty-four nations
met in San Francisco to discuss the treaty, and ultimately, forty-
seven of them signed it. Notable holdouts included the USSR,
Poland and Czechoslovakia, all of which objected to the promise to support the Republic of China and not do business with
the People's Republic of China that was forced on Japan by U.S.
politicians.

The rebuilding of Japan, principally by the United States, and the
good will exhibited on both sides help to explain the long and fruitful
relationship the people of these nations have enjoyed since 1945. Each
nation continues to support the other in political and military issues, with
barely a hint of disagreement or friction along the way. Japan is now fully
independent and a world power, but it continues to acknowledge the
value of the Americans who helped it to rise when the nation needed it
most.

TOYOTA ENTERS THE MODERN ERA

With his Koromo plant mostly restored (including gardens out back for growing crops for employees to eat) and with his workers concentrating on the trickle of orders for trucks to be used in the reconstruction, Kiichiro turned his thoughts once again to—what else?—cars. Koromo had been built to produce vehicles and to be distinct from the loom company. After the plant had been destroyed, the carmakers simply put on construction hats, rebuilt the factory, and then put their carmaker hats back on and started making vehicles again. This kind of communal response to hardship is itself an important part of what it means to be Japanese.

In postwar Japan, the era of the big, comfortable car was over almost before it began. The American influence prior to the war was to make full-powered, roomy vehicles on the Ford model. That style would never return. Now the only car that was appropriate for a devastated, shell-shocked people was a small, proper car, something that would not give offense or label its owner as a big spender when others were hungry.

Kiichiro rejected the thought of simply taking a big car and making it smaller. That was the problem with most of the vehicles now puttering around the city—they were underpowered and uncomfortable. The key was to start out with the idea of a small car and make it excellent. There was no reason that a small car could not be adequately powered, with an adequate wheelbase for turning, and show a little style at the same time.

The solution was to replace the heavy steel frame with a molded shell—at least in theory. Kiichiro and his engineers set to work turning theory into practice, but this conversion required a total reconfiguring of every component and every process. The result was the Model SA, in 1947. Its production name was Toyopet.

"TOYOPET IS YOUR PET!"

The SA was remarkable for many reasons.

First, Toyota designed it from the axles up to be Japan's car, the way the Volkswagen was Germany's car. It was not a knockoff of anything to do with Chevy or Ford. It was rethought, redesigned, refigured to be just what it was—the car for Japanese people.

Second, it was perfect for its time—it was 8 percent to 10 percent less expensive than anything the Americans could sell in Japan. During the reconstruction period, the people were thirsty for anything authentically Japanese, and the SA was it.

Third, it stayed on the road and refused to break down. Modern drivers take this sort of thing for granted, but having one's car break down or a tire blow out was a routine experience for car owners of every country until at least midcentury. It was especially true of Japan, where most of the roads and highways had been blasted with bombs during the war years, rendering many of them virtually impassable to all but high-water trucks. The SA sailed on by lesser vehicles, turning the old Toyota breakdown image on its head.

Fourth, it was irresistible. It was small, even for a two-door car, with only 27 horsepower. But it ran like a dream on wheels.

Fifth, the company spread the word of another public contest in the offing. The first one for a logo design had been a runaway hit. Now they were looking for a nickname for the SA. When the entries were judged, there was a clear winner: Toyopet.

Taken all together, it's why Toyota sold 100,000 vehicles that same year.

Best of all, Kiichiro was back in the car business.

On the home front, as well, there was a great deal of rebuilding to do. Backed by American financial aid and the universal desire to put the war behind them, the Japanese people set out to work with a will that has seldom been equaled anywhere. In several industries, including the automotive industry, American-style unions started forming—a decidedly un-Japanese concept to a people who saw harmony and mutual support as far better than confrontation and dissention. Japanese managers formerly were simply assumed to be patriotic and self-effacing. Now that the Americans were pulling the strings in the background, many citizens felt it was time to start looking after their own best interests.

The American influence leavened the entire culture. The occupiers had stores of their own, with massive window displays of the latest gadgets. The newspapers that the Americans left behind on benches and in trash bins showed advertisements for a dazzling array of goods— washing machines, pleasure-boat motors, suits and shoes of immense variety. And cars, whole flotillas of cars in a bewildering choice of styles and colors. American sailors and soldiers seemed to have unlimited wealth and spent it eagerly in the cities. This was the first time that regular citizens saw the Americans up close; they were awed at the trappings of wealth and power they displayed, in sharp contrast to the frugality that the Japanese culture demanded.

Kiichiro, in his usual counterpoint manner, looked east across the Pacific and saw a huge U.S. market ripe for picking. He had met hundreds of these people during his last tour of the country. He knew that not all of them were enamored of their gas-guzzling, road-hogging behemoths. The Americans were building cities like Chicago and San Francisco and Albany as tall and as fast as they could. Surely many of them would want a sporty urban car that could park anywhere and look, well, different.

With that as a long-range plan, he began building a network of dealerships across Japan. Times were hard, so he expected loyalty from the dealers and gave it in return. In really tough times he even went to the dealers for help with financing plant improvements. In the face of rampant inflation and then recession, with Toyota workers facing pay cuts and eventually layoffs, Kiichiro kept the fire of faith burning. We are in this together, he would say, and we will succeed together.

In fact, the times were too hard to overcome. Kiichiro had made promises to union leaders and to financing institutions that he felt he could no longer keep. He believed he had been tainted by all the events that were now crashing on his head. In May 1950, Kiichiro resigned as president of Toyota. He asked Taizo Ishida, president of Toyoda Automatic Loom Works, by far the most profitable company in the group, to take over for him. Ishida reluctantly agreed in the face of great personal regret that things had come to this. He said he would take over the reins of Toyota only until Kiichiro could regroup and the economic times got better.

Kiichiro must have smiled at the courtesy. In his mind, however, he knew that the idea of his return was not so farfetched. For the next two years he worked on new designs for a small car and began writing a book about his father's life. Shockingly, in March 1952, while working on the manuscript in a small inn, Kiichiro Toyoda suffered a massive cerebral hemorrhage and died. He was 57.

Americans Who Influenced Reconstruction in Japan after World War II

General Douglas MacArthur (1880–1964). General MacArthur applied his considerable ego and his world-class administrative skills to making Japan whole again. For years, he was the final authority on everything that happened in Japan. He promoted the idea of labor unions in the country to resist the growing threat of Communism, which had already taken over China. The historian David McCullough said: "There was nothing bland about him, nothing passive about him, nothing dull about him. There's no question about his patriotism, there's no question about his courage, and there's no question, it seems to me, about his importance as one of the protagonists of the Twentieth Century."

Joseph Dodge (1890–1964). A former chairman of The Detroit Bank, Dodge created an economic stabilization plan for Japan known as the Dodge Line. He cut off all government subsidies and stopped inflation in its tracks. His plan also caused widespread bankruptcy and led to the loss of hundreds of thousands of jobs.

W. Edwards Deming (1900–1993). Dr. Deming, known as the guru of quality control, is now a revered figure in Japan. A statistician by trade, he helped the United States improve the quality of its torpedoes during World War II. After the war, Japanese engineers invited him to come to Japan and work with them to change the international image of Japanese goods from shoddy to top quality. He predicted that they could do it in five years. In lectures in later years, he always got a laugh when he said that they did it in four.

Chapter Four

Strategies and Innovations

Americans carried on a love affair with their cars for 60 years.

They particularly admired the big eight-cylinder mammoths that cruised the smooth blacktop and concrete highways with hardly a bump to remind drivers that they were after all on land, not sea. The stately sedans of the 1930s and 1940s gave way to the tail-finned whales of the 1950s and 1960s, with their wide wheelbases and chromed beauty. Teenagers especially loved the cushioned bench seats in front that seemed made for romance at the drive-in movies. As the 1970s rolled in—along with the famous gas shortages and fuel price rises in 1974—the wide-waisted sofas on wheels yielded the right of way to the gas-miserly VW beetles and practical Toyotas that suburban moms used as taxis to the supermarket and train station. The love affair was over. It was time to settle down and get serious.

Kiichiro Toyoda had predicted all of it and had put all of his energies into designing and making a small, Japanese-style car.

By 1956, Toyota had established a large dealer chain for the Toyopet in Japan and had set up a small beachhead in California.

The Toyopet was launched in the United States with minimal fanfare, as if the company were slightly embarrassed at this modest offering from a modest carmaker. It was right to feel modest. The car was a spectacular failure. Toyota had hired a California public relations firm to help introduce the car to Americans, and the firm came up with one of the stupidest lines in advertising history: "Toyopet is YOUR pet!"

Americans laughed at the slogan and haughtily ignored the Toyopet. There was nothing American about it. The car was too small to get into comfortably. The steering wheel was too small. The foot pedals were too small. The radio dials were too small. The Ford Edsel—with its push-button shift mechanism in the center of the steering column and its clunky ride—would become the worst introduction of a new car in history; the Toyopet was next in line. Company managers pulled the car out of the market and retreated to Tokyo to rethink the entire vehicle, as well as their marketing strategy. Next time would be much different.

EIJI TOYODA TAKES THE TOUR

One of the strong business principles that Sakichi Toyoda had instilled into his company a generation ago had become legendary law by 1950: Study the best, and learn from them. It may be the foundational principle that resulted in Toyota's rise as the preeminent carmaker in the world. It was the motivation for both Sakichi and Kiichiro to buy looms and then automobiles from the finest producers in the world, take them apart down close to the molecular level, and study each part until they could duplicate it with their own machinery.

Just before wading ashore in America with their made-in-Japan cars, they sent their best scout: Eiji Toyoda. He was Kiichiro's cousin and made from the same mold: a brilliant young engineer, only 37 years old, a hard worker, and a firm believer that he was doing the right thing. Armed with a light suitcase and a few pens and notebooks, he set out for the New World in a haunting reprise of Kiichiro's visit just two decades before. American carmakers, just as they had for Kiichiro, threw open their doors for him, expecting that he had come to listen and observe and appreciate how efficient they were. He had come to do all those things; he had also come to learn how to beat them.

America in 1950 was very different for Eiji from the place that Kiichiro had visited before the war. The United States was in a consumer-driven frenzy. The troops had come back with money in their pockets and the GI Bill in their sea bags. They applied to college in vast numbers, married their old sweethearts (or even new ones), bought tract houses on the cheap, started families, and went on a spending spree like the world had never seen before.

Ford and GM and Chrysler and Oldsmobile didn't have to worry about making cars defect-free. Nobody cared about quality control. The American boys wanted lots of power and plenty of room. They wanted to take their girlfriends dancing on Saturday nights in style, so make those cars glitzy and bursting with chrome. The carmakers were selling cars just as fast as they could drive them off the line, and there was no end in sight.

Or perhaps the end was in sight; they just didn't notice him. Eiji came in a dark suit and white shirt and modest tie. He was polite and oh-so-grateful for the manufacturers' time. He asked a thousand questions and stopped only when his tour guide ran out of patience or time. And he took notes—reams of notes.

The carmakers, Eiji believed, had become fat and lazy. They couldn't make the cars fast enough, so why bother with improving quality? If the Ford Fairlane had an ongoing problem with the water pump, so what? If the sleek new Olds tended to wallow a bit in the rear when it hit 60 miles per hour, so what? If the famous Thunderbird vibrated on occasion, so what? Those returning GIs were spending like there would be no tomorrow, so let's make cars like there would be no tomorrow.

It was exactly the wrong attitude, and Eiji understood that immediately.

Ford's River Rouge plant, for example, when Kiichiro toured it, had been an overpowering gathering of men and metal in an ear-bursting clatter of noise and dust. But now, in 1950, Henry Ford had been dead for three years, and the cars his people were turning out were fancy on the outside but contained tired, out-of-date power trains on the inside. The industry now was glamour without substance. Eiji wrote it all down.

He toured every factory that would let him in and visited every state that would give him the time of day. The scale of the plants was tremendous—caverns of assembly lines and paint bays and shipping docks. But the equipment was old. Everybody seemed to be running on automatic. Nobody was thinking anymore; nobody was looking ahead and seeing the value of leanness and efficiency. Everyone behaved as if things would never change, as if Americans would always buy whatever cars Detroit wanted to make. The Edsel should have been a warning, but it wasn't. It was as if the Big Three were saying: "We're the carmakers, and you are the car buyers. Don't worry your heads about quality or gas mileage. Just trust us."

One valuable thing they were doing at Ford was to encourage "suggestion box" thinking. Any worker who had an idea about doing something better could write the idea on a slip of paper and be sure that management would see it. Who, after all, could see the potential for improvements better than the line worker? The culture at Ford was not known for wanting to hear from mere lunchbox workers. This particular development, however, is believed to have come from Henry Ford himself; no one dared criticize it. Once managers saw how effectively production could be improved with this system, they jumped aboard vigorously.

Eiji would implement this idea immediately in Japan, and it would become one of the two foundation stones for *kaizen*. (The other idea, one that Kiichiro Toyoda had borrowed from his tour of Ford plants, was the moving assembly line. He, too, had instituted this improvement the moment he returned to Japan, and it had created the potential for his famous just-in-time directive.)

In his mind, Eiji compared the production skills of the Americans with the workers he had back in Japan, and a profound hopefulness filled his spirit. We can do this! We can beat these people at their own game! We're already ahead of them technically and even mentally!

The situation was better than he knew at the time. Back home in Japan, the American reconstructionists were now distracted by the conflict between North and South Korea. They had decided to buy trucks in Japan rather than bring them in from the States. The Toyota plant, clogged with unsold trucks when he left, had now sold them all. The path was clear for cars once again. Once Eiji was aware of this, he set about planning for improved production processes. He also prepared a recommendation for the new president. The figure Eiji had in mind was staggering: 3,000 cars a month. One hundred cars a day. Eiji had another recommendation, as well. He had a man in mind who could put the plan into operation: Taiichi Ohno (ty-EE-chee OH-no).

Toyota's Mission

This is the mission statement of Toyota Motor Manufacturing North America:

1. As an American company, contribute to the economic growth of the community and the United States.
2. As an independent company, contribute to the stability and well-being of team members.
3. As a Toyota group company, contribute to the overall growth of Toyota by adding value to our customers.

One interesting aspect of this mission statement is that nowhere does it mention profits or continuing improvement or even the stockholders. In true Japanese style, it is concerned with the larger society, with doing the honorable thing to bring improvement to the lives of everyone—even those who have nothing to do with Toyota or its products.

Toyota's Guiding Principles

Anyone who thinks Toyota's North American mission statement is extraordinary should take a look at what Toyota calls its "Guiding Principles" within the company. The company published this document to employees, once Toyota had truly become a global manufacturing power, with the intent that all should understand Toyota's desire to be a good citizen *wherever* it operates.

1. Honor the language and spirit of the law of every nation and undertake open and fair corporate activities to be a good corporate citizen of the world.
2. Respect the culture and customs of every nation and contribute to economic and social development through corporate activities in the communities.
3. Dedicate ourselves to providing clean and safe products and to enhancing the quality of life everywhere through all our activities.
4. Create and develop advanced technologies and provide outstanding products and services that fulfill the needs of customers worldwide.
5. Foster a corporate culture that enhances individual creativity and teamwork value, while honoring mutual trust and respect between labor and management.

6. Pursue growth in harmony with the global community through innovative management.
7. Work with business partners in research and creation to achieve stable, long-term growth and mutual benefits, while keeping ourselves open to new partnerships.

One interesting aspect of these global principles is that they are uniquely Japanese. These could not have been sincerely written by a Chinese or German or American company, because those cultures care little for the "harmony" or "stability" of the indigenous workers in the countries in which these firms operate. American shoe companies in Indonesia, for example, and Scandinavian furniture companies in Mexico have little or nothing to say about such issues, preferring to leave them to local managers to implement as they see fit. Toyota codifies its principles in an effort to show local cultures that the Japanese way of doing things is to promote harmony or fail—to promote mutual respect or fail. Toyota sees this as a fair exchange because it asks nothing of locals that it does not ask of its own Japanese workers.

Another interesting aspect of the principles is that they reveal Toyota's desire from the start to be a global company. To build from the ground up for global expansion is to build wisely.

TOYOTA'S FIVE STRATEGIES FOR BECOMING THE NUMBER ONE CARMAKER

Strategy One: *Kaizen*—The Most Powerful Manufacturing Strategy on Earth

Kaizen is simple to translate: continuous improvement. But the simplicity is deceptive. Sakichi Toyoda, with his emphasis on making his looms better and better, can rightly be called the father of *kaizen*, at least as Toyota practices it. Kiichiro Toyoda made it his life's governing philosophy. Eiji Toyoda systematized it in vehicle production. And Taiichi Ohno gave it to the world. Many other companies neglect to take *kaizen* seriously, and those companies are not industry leaders. *Kaizen* is the single most important manufacturing philosophy in the world today.

If that is true, as I am convinced it is, why do so many companies refuse or neglect to practice it? The answer to that takes several forms.

First, *kaizen* is expensive in the short run. The Toyota practice of *kaizen* requires shutting down the production line whenever any significant breach of quality is detected. (This is an idea pioneered by Sakichi Toyoda for his automatic looms, where, if undetected, a malfunction could quickly cause a massive waste of thread.) Many manufacturers would rather fix defects at the end of the line—or send their defective products into the marketplace and hope for the best—than stop the line. In the long run, of course, *kaizen* is the optimum method for building profit.

Second, *kaizen* requires managers to give up the one thing that makes them superior to staff employees: information. The heart of *kaizen* is information sharing to the extent that even the lowliest, least-paid line worker knows everything important there is to know about the product at hand. Many managers, especially in the United States, are reluctant to share information that far, fearing that sharing of information is a loss of power. "If Joe Lunchbox down on the line," as managers might think to themselves, "knows as much about the product as I do, then who needs me?" It's a good question.

Third, *kaizen* is an Asian concept. It acknowledges the continuing existence of defects and problems—without assigning blame. Western manufacturers hate problems, and Western managers hate to be notified of problems. With many Western executives, their first thought on hearing about a problem is to ask who is to blame. The Japanese believe that the act of assigning blame itself is wasteful. It doesn't matter who is to blame. Often the system is to blame, not a person. So workers are encouraged to detect problems and are given bonuses when defects are fixed.

What, then, makes *kaizen* so crucial to success?

The answer is that *kaizen* is the overarching philosophy—the large tent—that protects all other Japanese management practices; indeed, it is what makes them possible in the first place.

Consider some of those management practices that were invented (or perfected) in Japan: total quality control, supportive labor relations, industrial robots, the suggestion box, lifetime employment, productivity studies, zero defects, and many others. None of these would work if it were not for the customer-focused environment that *kaizen* makes possible.

Kaizen is oriented completely toward process. Western manufacturing tends to be oriented toward profit. This dichotomy helps explain why so many profit-focused Western carmakers are struggling in the twenty-first century, while Toyota and other process-focused companies are prospering.

Take General Motors as one example. For generations, the autoworkers' unions have demanded higher wages and wider benefits, such as health care. The car companies went along with such demands in the past because the profits were there to pay for them. But when quality suffered and consumer demand fell, the unions were not sympathetic to losing benefits they had fought so hard to obtain. In August 2007, CNN reported that up to $1,800 in the price tag of a new American-made car goes to pay for health care and other benefits for autoworkers—some of whom retired years ago. Companies such as Toyota pay their workers fair wages and offer lifetime working opportunities but do not have the far-reaching benefits that are so costly to American carmakers. It's like racing against an opponent who is dragging a 90-pound weight.

Kaizen is a uniquely Japanese mindset. It says that if something is important—a relationship, an automatic loom, a university, an automobile— then there should be some kind of improvement in it somewhere every day. One looks for problems and feels joy to find them, because a problem is merely notification that something specific needs improving. A problem is how a potential improvement raises its hand and says, "Here I am."

This philosophy is innately Japanese, of course, but it is available to anyone who wishes to adopt it. Take Tiger Woods, for example. Mr. Woods is certainly one of the greatest golfers in history and possibly the best of all time. His golf swing is legendary for its smooth rhythm and kinetic power. Most golfers would instantly swap their swing for his, if given the chance. But in 2005, Tiger Woods decided to *kaizen* his golf swing. He took crucial time off from the professional tour and rebuilt his swing from the ground up. Many commentators were unimpressed by his announcement. Why take a risk by changing your swing when it's already the best in the world? Mr. Woods came back to the tour with his new swing and his *kaizen* attitude and started breaking records that had stood for generations. Anything can be improved, even the perfect golf swing of Tiger Woods.

Interestingly, Mr. Woods put aside his quest for *profit* temporarily in order to concentrate on *process*. In *kaizen* management theory, this must happen in corporations, as well, even those that are founded on securing profit for their shareholders. Profit is the enemy of *kaizen*. Profit demands the making of money now. *Kaizen* demands the continuing improvement of process, even when it costs money. In the Toyota management ranks today, when there is a conflict between profit and *kaizen*, *kaizen* always wins. In the late 1940s, forgoing profit in order to improve the process was a high-risk gamble that no one was sure would pay off.

Many observers feel that *kaizen* was born in the ashes of World War II. In those early days, the challenge was simply to stay alive. In the 1950s, it was to recover enough to begin to compete with others who did not have to start over and who did not have to rebuild their houses at night while they built cars during the day. In the 1960s, the challenge was to make people forget the jokes about "made in Japan" and start thinking about high quality and attention to detail. In other words, the true challenge was progress every day. And so *kaizen* became the way to stay alive.

Now *kaizen* is Toyota's long-term path for productivity and profitability. Twenty years ago, Eiji Toyoda put it this way: "One of the features of the Japanese workers is that they use their brains as well as their hands. Our workers provide one and a half million suggestions a year, and 95 percent of them are put to practical use. There is an almost tangible concern for improvement in the air at Toyota."

To Americans, the emphasis has always been on reaching the destination, whether it's traveling from Cleveland to Omaha or building the Erie Canal. Enjoying the journey is not nearly as important as getting there, wherever "there" is. It's how you move an entire civilization west across 3,000 miles, building roads and cities along the way. In Japanese culture, the emphasis has always been on experiencing the journey. The point of the elaborate tea ceremony is not to drink tea but to drink tea properly, respectfully, and so to showcase one's adherence to social constructs—to show that one is mindful of one's place in the grand scheme.

Kaizen speaks directly to the Japanese understanding of human nature. Let's say American Worker Smith's job is to assemble a Framitz "Delta" hub (whatever that is!) and connect it to both the front and rear axle of a unit on the production line. Smith has been doing this for two years and is quite skilled at it. Now let's say he has an idea. As a skilled worker, he can assemble the Framitz hubs faster than Worker Clark, who is relatively unskilled. His idea is to assemble only the hubs and then pass them to Clark, who simply bolts them onto the axles. This uses two workers rather than one, yes, but in a year's time Smith figures this improvement will result in the production of 1,500 additional units and add more than $1 million to company sales. Does he take his idea to the supervisor? No. For several reasons.

One, two workers cost more than one, no matter how you do the math. Smith wants to add additional labor costs up front to increase the bottom line a year from now. The company wants to be profitable now. Next year will have to take care of itself.

Two, the supervisor would never take such an idea upstairs to the managers. Supervisors are rated on results. Smith is performing the two functions well, and why should anyone mess with success? Additionally, Smith's idea would require reconfiguring the line. Others would see the benefits and would want their tasks reconfigured, as well. Soon enough, the unions would step in and insist that any change requires raising the salary.

Three, the senior managers would likely conclude that Smith is getting lazy and is looking for some help so that he can take longer breaks. They would instruct the supervisor to watch Smith more closely and ensure that he maintains his production schedule. They would also begin to question the supervisor's judgment in failing to consider the chaos that follows any change in procedures.

Western manufacturing systems are based on results; Japanese systems are based on process. These are diametrically opposite ways of looking at the universe. They speak to ancient cultural and even geographical differences. The West—particularly the United States—developed out of abundance. There was never a need to be frugal. For example, the British and French adventurers who landed on North America's eastern shore discovered ocean-like expanses of forests ripe for cutting. They needed wood for masts and ships and houses and so hewed down whole forests without heed for future needs.

When profit is the main motive, it's no wonder that so many manufacturing plants have remained unchanged over dozens of years. Change is always expensive. Even when undertaken, it may or may not result in increased profits.

Japanese culture developed from scarcity. There was never enough of anything—rice, wood, wheat, oil, human labor—to even think about the possibility of waste. The only life-saving action was to improve constantly, to take what little you have and make more of it than anyone else could.

Both cultures are aiming toward success and profit. One has the luxury of demanding results, and one has no option but to improve the process. In the long run, of course, improving process is clearly the better option because waste—even in the midst of abundance—will eventually catch up and pull you down. That's part of what happened to Western car making in the twentieth century, and it helps explain why so many Western manufacturers are now trying to catch up to the benefits of *kaizen.*

In any *kaizen* system, managers and supervisors drive the action. Unlike a results-oriented manager, whose job is to issue orders and punish offenders, the process manager stimulates and supports the workers' efforts to improve the system. This requires a far different set of skills. Stimulating and supporting both take time and effort. Teaching is more difficult than merely giving orders and expecting obedience. *Kaizen* looks to the front-line worker to detect and mend problems. It expects the supervisor to support a worker's desire to stop the line or otherwise inhibit the product flow. By extension, *kaizen* is an investment in people. Machines break down or wear out. Technology supplants old ways with new ones. But people are constant. Their nature doesn't change, and their desire to improve is nourished by a supervisor's desire to support that improvement.

In *kaizen,* if workers are the key, supervisors are the power source.

Taiichi Ohno and the Chalk Circle

Ohno came to Toyota in the middle of World War II, when the military was running shop operations. They had combined the textile and car companies into one, with the inevitable unhappy result. The textile operation was by now smooth running and profitable. Profits were based on volume, and so the workers were geared for maximum speed. Japanese textiles were competing quite well with those of all other textile companies around the world.

The car operation was the opposite in every way. It was thoroughly outdistanced by even minor Western carmakers.

Ohno's challenge as a young engineer was to bring the two operations together so that they might work efficiently. His first order of business was to do what Sakichi Toyoda himself had done so well so long ago with his mother's hand loom: observe. The phrase in Japanese is *genchi genbutsu shugi:* learn through careful observation at the site. This is now a companywide slogan at today's Toyota.

Ohno was well known for his imaginative teaching methods. When he encountered a worker or supervisor who was stumped as to why something wasn't working, he drew a chalk circle on the floor and asked the person to stand in it and observe until the answer became clear. It almost always worked.

You can easily try this yourself. For example, stand quietly and un-obtrusively near a supermarket checkout line. Observe the action. Can you think of ways to help the lines move faster? Most supermar-kets have express lanes (12 items or fewer) that are frequently empty. Would it help to put a green light, say, at the express lane that would invite one shopper with more than 12 items to step in? Would it help to have a cash-only line? What causes most bottlenecks? Is any time wasted looking for the price of an unmarked item? And so on. It might be a fun experiment that would certainly demonstrate the power of observation. People can't fix a problem until they know what is really causing it.

Years ago, the makers of Surf laundry detergent had a problem. They were losing market share to the big names like Tide and Cheer. At the time, the big brands were running television commercials say-ing that their soap helped clothes get whiter than white! and brighter than bright! People needed sunglasses just to do the laundry.

So Surf sent researchers out to hundreds of laundromats across the United States to observe normal people washing their clothes. How do you think normal people determine whether their clothes are clean? By observing them in the light for brightness?

No. They smell them.

Normal people smell their clothes to discover if they are clean or not. This was a true "chalk circle" breakthrough! Surf added 12 per-cent more perfume to its detergent than the big brands had, and within six months Surf had become a big brand, too.

Genchi genbutsu shugi!

Your experiment in *kaizen* doesn't actually have to contain a chalk circle (see sidebar). What's important is the *kaizen* attitude. A famous and classic example of a manager with a *kaizen* attitude involves Roger Enrico and one of the world's most popular brand names: Doritos chips. In this case, Mr. Enrico didn't stand in a chalk circle—he sat at his desk.

Mr. Enrico, in 1973, was a young brand manager at Frito-Lay in Dal-las, Texas, in charge of the Doritos brand. At the time, Doritos came in just three flavors: original Toasted Corn, Taco, and Nacho Cheese.

Nacho Cheese, the newest, was selling well, but the company rolled the numbers for all the flavors into the total Doritos brand. He asked his advertising agency, Tracy-Locke, in Dallas, to give him data on the trial rate of all three. (A trial rate is the percentage of customers who are trying your product for the first time.)

The agency delved into painstaking research for more than two months, crunching the numbers into ever-finer data. Finally, the results were in: Toasted Corn and Taco both had a trial rate of 40 percent. Nacho Cheese came in at just 10 percent. Mr. Enrico scratched his head. How could this be? Nacho Cheese had a trial rate one-quarter that of the other two flavors, and yet its sales were the same. He sat at his desk looking at the research, and the hairs started to stand up on the back of his neck. If sales were the same with just a quarter of the trial rate, then Nacho Cheese was a massive hit! If the other two flavors were hitting inside-the-park home runs, Nacho Cheese was knocking the ball across town!

It can't be true, he thought to himself. It can't be this easy. Something's wrong somewhere. He had the ad agency run the numbers all over again from scratch. The result was exactly the same.

Roger Enrico went into full-*kaizen* mode. He ordered Tracy-Locke to relaunch Nacho Cheese as a stand-alone brand. He took his case to the boardroom and persuaded his bosses to run television and radio commercials featuring only Nacho Cheese—something the company had never done before. Within a year, sales doubled. Frito-Lay now dominates the salty snacks category the way Intel and Microsoft dominate their categories and is just as profitable. Can you guess the biggest moneymaking product within Frito-Lay? Nacho Cheese Doritos.

Kaizen philosophy as practiced by Toyota teaches us that true excellence results when we do two things well. First, we have to get our hands dirty, put our stomachs on the floor, if we have to, and see what there is to see. Second, we have to apply the power of human imagination to the problem and see what develops.

Observation, then action—it's the heart of *kaizen*.

Here's another case to illustrate the point. The supervisor of the waitresses at a Japanese company's cafeteria made it clear that she supported Quality Control (QC) at every level, from ordering food to preparing month-end accounting data. She formed the women into teams (another *kaizen* tactic) and said that the winners would receive a big award (yet another *kaizen* tactic).

One team considered the consumption of tea during lunch. Tea was not a considerable expense, but it was an *expense,* just the same. *Kaizen* philosophy makes no distinction between big or small—everything helps and everything can be improved.

Company policy was to put a large pot of tea at each table and let the diners help themselves. The waitresses stood in their own imaginary chalk circles and observed several things.

One, people tended to sit at the same table every day.

Two, tea consumption varied greatly from table to table. Some tables consumed the whole pot, but some consumed little, causing waste. In *kaizen,* waste is a delightful problem to have, because you can fix waste.

The women collected data for weeks and found they could predict with great accuracy what each table's consumption would be. With these findings in hand, they began putting differing levels of tea in each pot. Soon they had cut the cafeteria's tealeaf purchases in half and saved—not much money. So what? *Kaizen* cares about process, and they had detected and eradicated waste. They won the Presidential Gold Medal that year.

That, in a tealeaf, is *kaizen.*

Kaizen Thinking	Results Thinking
Long term	Short term
Small improvements	Big innovations
Small steps	Huge steps
Unrestricted	Limited
People oriented	Technology oriented
Team heroes	Individual heroes
Gradual, smooth	Abrupt, volcanic
Maintain/improve	Scrap/rebuild
Process	Profits
Invest in process	Invest in equipment
Works best in slow economic conditions	Works best in fast-growing economic conditions
Conventions	Inventions

There is an old saying in the aircraft manufacturing industry that "if it's flying, it's obsolete." The time from designing an airplane to rolling it out of the hangar is so vast that often the people who started the process are retired by the time it is completed. Similarly, in economics, Parkinson's Law states that "work expands to fill the time available for it." The law explains why virtually no complex projects are completed before the due date. Systems are the output of human nature, and human nature never changes. People will do what they are rewarded for doing. If they are rewarded for finding problems and fixing them, they will do that. If they are rewarded for focusing on the end product and ignoring problems if possible, they will do that.

Kaizen theory fits in nicely here as well, as it helps us to deal with the world as it really is. Simply put, most organizational systems are designed to maximize the technology as it exists when the system is designed. By definition, then, this means that organizational systems start *deteriorating* the moment they have been set in place. If you set the system up and then walk away from it to enjoy profits, you are determining the system's ultimate failure. Keeping the system current and up to the minute requires ongoing effort from everyone involved, line workers to managers. The economies of mass production will not be around to maintain and improve this system. *Kaizen* will.

Two good modern examples are UPS and Federal Express. Both companies suggest that when their first automated distribution centers were opened for business, they were already out of date. New facilities were already in the works.

No organization can remain static, yet many of them continue to do business as if stasis were the reality. *Kaizen* suggests that employees must continually improve the process simply to stay in place. To move forward in time requires heavy-duty reliance on minute-by-minute improvement.

Surgeons report that new procedures and anesthesia medications have rendered obsolete even recent breakthroughs. Web-based commerce is capable of tracking and servicing new customers in ways that were unavailable even in 2006! Global Positioning Systems (GPS) are being used to find lost children and pinpoint hidden "geocache" treasures down to a 14-inch circle.

This kind of astonishing innovation is the gold standard of Western manufacturing. The West tends to wait and hope for a dramatic innovation that will radically change and (one hopes) improve how things are done now. The fly in the ointment is obvious: Even this dramatic new performance level will begin declining the moment it is introduced. Unless someone begins immediately to add constant improvements to it, today's brilliant innovation will become yesterday's old news. Innovation is dramatic and one-time-only. *Kaizen* is ongoing and cumulative.

As innovations keep piling up, the industrial landscape begins to move by in a blur. *Kaizen* is the only industrial method capable of keeping up. It remains the best explanation we have for why Toyota is now the most successful carmaker on planet Earth. In 2007 Toyota produced 213,000 more automobiles than General Motors, making Toyota the leader in global vehicle production for the first time (Kageyama, 2008). In the first quarter of 2008, Toyota sold 160,000 more vehicles worldwide than GM (Krisher, 2008).

The Five Whys

Early on, leaders of the Toyota Motor Company developed a simple system for analyzing problems and making decisions. They call it the Five Whys. Ask five good questions about a problem, and chances are you will discover its source.

Taiichi Ohno often gave the following example of how engineers can work together to find the actual cause of a problem. In this example, he examines a machine breakdown.

Q1: Why did the machine stop?
A1: Because the fuse blew due to an overload.
Q2: Why was there an overload?
A2: Because the bearing lubrication was inadequate.
Q3: Why was the lubrication inadequate?
A3: Because the lubrication pump was not functioning right.
Q4: Why wasn't the lubrication pump working right?
A4: Because the pump axle was worn out.
Q5: Why was it worn out?
A5: Because sludge got in.

When you ask the five whys, you tend to get the real answer. The engineer could have simply replaced the fuse and gone on with his work, only to be interrupted again when the new fuse blew. With the Five Whys system, the engineer will now put a strainer on the lubrication pump, then replace the fuse, then get on with the work with the likelihood that there will be no more interruptions caused by a blown fuse.

Strategy Two: Just in Time

When Kiichiro Toyoda tacked up the sign in the shop that said "Just in Time," he was not thinking that the concept would change the world of manufacturing or make Toyota a dominant carmaker within 50 years. He was trying to make his little shop floor more efficient.

"Be careful in the little things," the old saying goes, "and the big things will take care of themselves." Kiichiro's concentration on the little details would have great rewards...down the road.

The challenge that Kiichiro faced was rooted in the basic reality of smallness. He had no room for storage and so had to come up with some other way. In other words, he had to start small because there was no other choice. Another challenge presented itself almost from the start. He had to produce a limited number of different cars and trucks to meet the differing needs of his customers.

He didn't think this was remarkable until he stepped inside Henry Ford's River Rouge plant in Detroit and gazed in wonder at the massive conveyor belt systems that brought the cars to the workers. This was manufacturing on the scale of the pyramids! Kiichiro didn't realize it at the time, perhaps, but the Ford moving assembly line was a nascent just-in-time operation. Even here, where the roof-covered line went on seemingly for miles, there was room only for a small collection of components. Where workers labored side by side in the dust and noise, the area to store parts was minimal. So Ford had developed a crude system to keep the piles of parts stocked. It wasn't pretty, but it worked well enough.

As far as Ford was concerned, this small stockpiling was vital to profits for one simple reason: The customers demanded low prices, and low prices they would have. The bargain Ford Motor Company made with the world was elegant in its simplicity. We will make an affordable car, the bargain stated, so long as you will accept one shape, one color (black), and the once-in-a-while need to fix or replace defective parts. If you, the customer, will agree to accept exactly the vehicle we produce, with no custom additions, we will keep the price low enough that even farmers and shopkeepers can afford it.

It was a bargain that made the Ford Motor Company wealthy beyond dreams and put ordinary Americans on the road, traveling from here to there in a style and a timeframe that would have made earlier kings and queens seethe with jealousy.

The dream lasted for two generations, until the World War II soldiers came home and started to demand green or blue instead of black, and two doors instead of four, and by the way would you make the steel roof a rag-top? Now Ford's crude stockpiling system broke down, and Kiichiro's early just-in-time idea was turned into a manufacturing process that changed the world.

Visitors to Toyota's Motomachi plant are treated to a sight that Henry Ford would have understood and admired immediately. Trucks—a long line of trucks—are lined up at the receiving docks of the plant like pilgrims come to worship at a small shrine. The trucks contain a wide variety of components and parts destined for the assembly line. As soon as one truck is offloaded, it drives away, and another takes its place. This is the part that would have made Henry Ford wish he had thought of it: The trucks are the warehouse!

Business commentators often call the Toyota production system *nonstock*. However, it's not exactly the case. Workers always have some level of stock at hand to help smooth out any gaps in delivery. But the heart of what makes Toyota work well is that most of the time, when a worker puts out his hand to retrieve an item, it is there as if by magic. If one considers exquisite planning magic, then Toyota is happy to go along with it.

The true magic of the system is in the imagination of Taiichi Ohno, who developed the modern technology for economically manufacturing a variety of automobiles on the same production line. If Henry Ford made the production line move, then Taiichi Ohno made it customer focused.

Ohno built his process on the concept of waste. He is against waste of any kind. He sees the elimination of waste as the key to *kaizen* and just-in-time efficiency. He once classified production waste into seven categories.

- Overproduction
- Wasted machine time
- Transportation waste
- Processing waste
- Taking inventory
- Inefficient motion
- Defective components

The main villain in all of this, according to Ohno, is overproduction.

In Western manufacturing, one reduces cost by keeping the line rolling. Let's say, by way of example, that we are manufacturing marshmallow and peanut (M&P) candy bars. We keep production costs down by never stopping the line. Let's further say that demand for our M&P candy bars falls away in Pittsburgh. Those darn Pittsburghians have decided in their wisdom that they prefer marshmallow and almond (M&A) candy bars. Doesn't matter to us. We keep that line rolling and figure we'll either warehouse the extra M&Ps or else discount them steeply. The most expensive thing we can do is stop that line. Why? Because we have massive vats of marshmallow and peanuts and must get them into production or they will spoil, effectively destroying our profit margin.

If we were following a just-in-time system, however, it wouldn't matter if demand falls in Pittsburgh. We have trucks backing up to our receiving docks with marshmallow and peanuts that we have ordered *on the basis of demand*. When Pittsburghians start buying those M&As, that's what we order from suppliers.

When the trucks become our warehouse, we can produce on the basis of actual customer orders and not of predictions of what customers might order.

Another key to Toyota's success in this area is its training of vendors and subcontractors to buy into the system as well. Just-in-time production requires the mastery of hundreds of conductors directing thousands of musicians at the same time in order to be profitable. If the violin section in just one orchestra is just two beats behind all the others, the audience leaves and profits fade away.

One other important concept deserves mention in connection with just-in-time: *jidohka*. This term has been cleverly translated as *autonomation* (distinct from automation, which means doing the exact same machine task over and over). In autonomation, the emphasis is on "no." Toyota builds its machines with automatic stop mechanisms. That is, the machine is designed to stop instantly whenever it detects a malfunction of any kind. So, at any Toyota plant, a defect in the work shuts down the entire line. This sounds expensive, and it is, but there are economies built in.

We've already discussed how the discovery of a problem is a cause for joy in Japanese manufacturing philosophy. In *jidohka*, the joy comes twice.

First, it comes from finding a problem and fixing it so thoroughly that it will not recur. Fixing a small problem upstream is far more economical in the long run than fixing a big problem downstream. How expensive is it, for example, for a car manufacturer to recall half a million vehicles in order to fix a defect in the fan-belt housing? The answer: You don't want to know.

Second, there is an even larger economy having to do with workers. If your machines are designed to detect defects and shut down, that means you can spread your workforce across many more machines. The economies here are staggering, considering that employee compensation is among the largest overhead items for any manufacturer.

Speaking of overhead, all Toyota plants have large electronic signboards attached to the ceiling throughout the workspace. When a machine stops, the sign lights up with its number, and specially trained maintenance people gladly rush to repair it and restart the line.

Because making vehicles is so massively complex, there is plenty of "joy" to go around all day long.

Once again, *kaizen* is the heart of this system. One cannot put a just-in-time framework in place for production and walk away. It requires intense concentration and exacting focus on every detail to work. But if you can make it work, you can lead the world.

Strategy Three: The Suggestion System

Consider New York City as a model of what Toyota does around the world every day. New York has a mayor, a police force, a city hall, and a bevy of managers who oversee the hundreds of services the city provides every day, from street cleaning to subway transportation. But what really makes New York City work, what really compels millions of visitors a year to come see for themselves what the millions of city dwellers are raving about, is the way its citizens micromanage their own affairs.

The art gallery manager in SoHo, the deli cook in midtown, the television producer on the West Side, the hotel bookkeeper on the East Side, the Wall Street attorney—they are all minding their own business quite well. They are not trying to feed and house and entertain millions of people a day; they are trying to work with the things they know on a much smaller scale. New York City works because nearly everyone concentrates to maintain his or her piece of the action.

In the same way, Toyota bases its *kaizen* program on the attention-to-detail of every employee and every work team. Their principal tool for doing this is the suggestion system.

When Eiji Toyoda visited the Ford plants in 1950, he closely studied the manner in which line workers conscientiously filled out forms for the "suggestion box." Mr. Ford himself had been an advocate of the suggestion system since the 1930s, and that ensured that every supervisor was an advocate, as well. Some of the suggestions were grievance- or personality-related, and subject to being ignored. But many were tight recommendations from people who got their hands dirty actually doing the work. Until his death, in 1947, Mr. Ford claimed that he read each suggestion and passed a good number of them down the line for action.

Eiji liked the system, as well. He saw instantly that no one on earth knows the task better than the worker performing it. Henry Ford probably liked the fact that he was receiving inputs on improving the line for free. Eiji Toyoda liked the idea of turning every line worker into a QC expert. Back in Japan, his company was facing waves of red ink while people were trying to rebuild the devastated landscape. He was looking for any idea that worked, and the suggestion box worked.

Typically, Toyota improved on Ford's system with a formal policy that paid cash bonuses to anyone whose suggestion was put into practice. In the 1960s, this system was considered a success when employees contributed an average of 2.5 suggestions per person per year.

In 1973, a global oil shortage savaged the automobile industry as well as the economic stability of many nations. Drivers from Philadelphia to

Paris to Stockholm waited hours in line at gas stations just to fill up. In Japan, where nearly 100 percent of the oil is imported, prices per gallon rose nearly 60 percent. Raw materials such as leather and steel went up in similar increments. The bottom dropped out of car sales, and all manufacturers were scrambling for any ideas to help save costs. Now the 3 ideas per worker increased to 10. Best of all, most of the ideas had to do with cutting costs, cutting wastes, and increasing efficiencies.

Today, Toyota's global suggestion system results in hundreds of thousands of improvements every year, from the arrangement of a work team on the production floor to the quality of soap in the rest rooms. More impressive still, Toyota accepts and considers implementing more than 90 percent of the suggestions. And the cash awards still apply, from about $5 up to around $2,000 per idea.

If you ever get to tour a Toyota plant, you'll be amazed at the elevated mobile chairs and synchronized dollies—both the result of worker suggestions. The convertible top on the Camry Solara that used to take more than half an hour to install has been *kaizen*ed to about eight minutes. It will probably take around six minutes to install by the time you take the tour.

The Deming Wheel

In the early days after the devastation of World War II, most Japanese companies had to start over from the ground up. The United States, because it had nearly destroyed the country, felt an obligation to send in experts to help the rebuilding efforts. One such expert was W. Edwards Deming, a scientist whose specialty was studying the statistical methods of quality control (QC). In Japan, he set to work on controlling quality by improving inspection methods.

Most producers of products inspected the units at the end of the production line in order to discard defective ones. Deming believed this was wasteful and nearly useless. What if a defective machine up the line was ruining the quality of *all* of the products? He instituted two reforms to improve this picture.

One, every worker on the factory floor should be responsible for checking and controlling the quality of each unit, even if it meant shutting down the line.

Two, to be truly useful the program had to involve every person in the company who drew a paycheck, and not just the floor workers. Deming called this system TQC, or Total Quality Control. TQC is now as ubiquitous worldwide among manufacturers as are laptop computers and e-mail. In Japan in the late 1950s, however, no one else was doing this. In fact, no one else around the world could be bothered. Most producers were trying their best to speed up the process, not slow it down for some vague (they thought) notion of *quality,* whatever that was supposed to mean.

It sounds absurd to talk about this today, where high quality is the minimum cost of getting into the game. Anyone over 40 can attest to the fact that virtually every new car—even a low-priced compact—coming off any production line in the world is likely to be of better quality than expensive cars were back in the 1970s. People who were old enough to drive in the 1950s can remember when tires routinely blew out for no apparent reason, leaving cars stranded at the side of the road like wounded ducks. I suspect that most drivers under 30 today have never seen a car with a flat tire. The quality of most products is now extremely high, from circuit breakers to circus tents. For Deming, however, postwar Japan was the only audience at the time interested in his ideas about improving quality. When Japanese products started outselling and outperforming all other products in the world, the rest of the world started to take notice. For many of them, however, it was a case of too little, too late.

Deming himself has called this tool the *Shewhart Cycle,* named after Bell Laboratories scientist Walter Shewhart, the statistician who also developed statistical process control in the 1930s.

The Deming Wheel has come to be called PDCA: Plan—Do—Check—Act. Deming stressed that continuous improvement had to be organization-wide or it would have no effect at all. In order for a company to provide the best possible products or services for its customers, it would have to coordinate among research, design, production, and sales. He sketched it out this way:

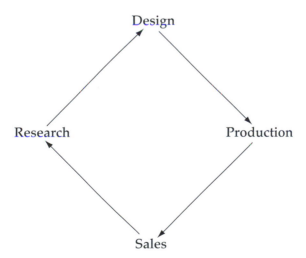

The Deming Wheel allows for each of the four elements of manufacturing to drive the action at some point in the process.

Each was tied to the other, and each was responsible for passing on the highest level of quality to the next department in line. He further stressed that the wheel should rotate on the basis of satisfying the most immediate requirements.

Plan: Have a strategy for completing the work.
Do: Complete the work on the basis of the plan.
Check: Have you satisfied the plan with your work?
Act: What must you do to improve the work or move to the
             next stage?

In theory, the Wheel increases your long-term prospects for success, rather than your simply reacting to problems as they crop up. Often an immediate and dramatic improvement is simply not possible. But PDCA can improve any process—even incrementally—over time. Its real strength is in incremental and continuous *kaizen*-style process improvements. Deming intended for practitioners to use it as a guide to analyze processes.

Even today the Deming Wheel is often misunderstood. Typically, Western companies use it to keep production-floor workers in line but fail to implement it throughout the organization. Toyota is not one of those companies.

Strategy Four: The *Kanban* System

Kanban is a Japanese idiom that can mean a number of things, depending on context. Think of a laminated clipboard and you'll be close, at least in one context. *Kanban* mostly means "door plate" or "sign plate," but that's not as helpful as its other potential meanings of an empty bin or empty cart or blank ticket. *Kanban*, in essence, is a signal or trigger that alerts workers upstream, telling them that something needs to be replenished downstream. Which brings us to supermarkets.

Taiichi Ohno became fascinated with American supermarkets in the 1950s, when they had just begun to replace the old mom-and-pop markets on street corners. (The southern chain Piggly Wiggly was among his favorites.) The economies of scale meant that supermarkets could significantly underprice the corner store and still be profitable. When Japan imported the idea, he became a true student of the supermarket and studied them all intensely. In fact, in later years he spoke of iron and steel "rotting" in storage areas. He meant not that the metals were ripening and going bad, of course, but that their languishing unused signaled a kind of waste that was burning up money.

What inspired him was that a supermarket is entirely "customer pulled." That is, customers determine when the shelves or bins need restocking. The market manager does not rely totally on a prescribed schedule—if it's Tuesday, it must be time to deliver more tomatoes. Not at all. That is a kind of "push" marketing style that all the auto manufacturers were doing at the time. The suppliers pushed the components into the receiving area of the factory, and the workers—under pressure from the back room—pushed finished products out the delivery end. That kind of thinking is fine in a heated economy where one can't sell product fast enough. In a cooled economy, push marketing can spell economic disaster, with paid-for components piling up in corners and "rotting."

The grocer's thinking is, rather, like this: If the tomato bin is nearly empty, then I'll order more for delivery this afternoon and let the customers pull those out the door, as well. Once in a while, however, if a bin is empty, a customer has to wait or do without. In the long run, that's a better tradeoff than stockpiling goods that do not sell. A supermarket is a true just-in-time system because many of the products a store sells are perishable. (This analogy is not nearly as compelling in the modern era, when so much produce can be frozen or refrigerated to extend its useful life.) The manager does not have the luxury of hoping that customers will buy according to schedule. If his produce and milk and eggs don't sell, they will spoil. He has already paid for them. So spoilage means that the manager has wasted his money.

The notion of perishability is a fact of life for many modern organizations. Commercial airlines, for example, try to sell unused seats just before takeoff at rock-bottom prices or else those seats will "perish." Newspapers must sell the day they are printed; nobody buys yesterday's paper.

That was the key for Ohno—perishability. Steel can perish, too! Iron can perish, too! Leather for seat covers is perishing if it is not used and instead is stored, wasting space and capital. Perishability moved him more than any other concept to pin Toyota's future on just-in-time thinking.

And that's where *kanban* comes in. It's a pre-computer concept still in use at Toyota worldwide because it works beautifully. The essence of *kanban* is simplicity. Visitors to Toyota plants are always dazzled by the colorful *kanban* cards or bins flying this way or that. It's like looking into a microscope and seeing blood carry oxygen and nutrients to various parts of the body as they need them. Because that's exactly what *kanban* does.

Ohno needed a foolproof way to signal (to "pull") parts or components from where they had been waiting briefly to become installed on the line. How to accomplish that? What should the trigger be? When a worker downstream needs a part, he signals the workers upstream with a *kanban* and pulls the part down to him. The *kanban* trigger is virtually foolproof. Over time, worker suggestions have resulted in many small improvements, from laminating certain *kanbans* to color-coding them.

When a part is used, the worker can send the *kanban* back upstream as a record of what part was used and as an order for a new one. Toyota has found that the *kanban* system is an ideal adjunct to its just-in-time philosophy in several ways. For one, it reduces communication time between stations. For another, it prevents most problems because the status of a part is clear and instantly observable. Plant visitors often ask tour guides why Toyota uses a nonelectronic system for such important communications. When we can improve it, the guide usually says, we will.

That's exactly the right answer, from the company that invented *kaizen.*

Strategy Five: Ask Your Customers

We make things everybody thinks we should make.

—Katsuaki Watanabe, president,
Toyota Motor Corporation

Many successful companies understand intuitively that customers are more than passengers on board their ships. Customers provide the propulsion, decide what course to take, and also steer the ship. And, once in a while, when the mood strikes them, customers abandon one ship for another.

Oldsmobile, in the late 1980s, understood that it was losing its younger customers to Toyota, among others. So it put some minor stylistic changes onto the smaller models and proudly announced that the new car now in showrooms was "not your father's Oldsmobile." Yes, it was, the youngsters decided, and they abandoned ship. They never returned. Instead, they bought Toyotas.

Twenty years later, the Big Three seemed to have learned little about the care and feeding of customers. In a 1996 press conference announcing a higher-than-expected sticker price for the Ford Taurus, the executive in charge became irritated at the reporters who kept wondering why the cost was so high. "If Joe Blow can't afford a new car, that's tough," the executive said. "Let him go buy a used car." Joe Blow evidently didn't care for a used car or a loudmouthed executive or an overpriced American car. He bought a Toyota.

A bare 13 years earlier, General Motors had come out swinging with a big colorful cover on *Fortune* magazine that featured its hottest four sedans ever. GM claimed that the Chevy Celebrity, Pontiac 6000, Buick Century, and Olds Cutlass Ciera would be the new kings of the car-buying mountain. Customers looked at the photo and saw the same car in four different flavors—underpowered, featureless, sexless flavors. They bought a few of these mediocrities—this was GM, after all, the biggest car company in the world—but many of them bought Toyotas.

Nobody has a lock on customers. They are famously fickle. They decided against 8-track tapes and Schlitz beer. They decided the Edsel was too weird. They decided that New Coke was nowhere near as pleasing as the old Coke. They decided that CD players were not nearly as cool as iPods. They decided that flat-screen LCD TVs were the only way to go. And so it goes.

Sometimes customers will go along with a manufacturer's arrogance if it's in their best interests to do so. "You can have a car in any color you want," Henry Ford said in 1919, "as long as it's black." Customers went along with it because they were eager to get on the road and the Tin Lizzie could get them there. Customers rule. In attending to all the myriad details of getting good-quality products to market at a fair price, companies sometimes forget that eternal truth. Good companies recover and get back to pleasing the real boss, the customer.

Even Toyota has yielded to the temptation of listening to its own internal experts rather than asking customers what they want. In 1999, it tried to attract younger and edgier customers—a demographic decidedly not in Toyota's core market. Mohawk-sporting snowboarders were not interested in driving Corollas, reliable and economical as they were. So the company came out with three models designed expressly for these younger, flashier drivers: the Celica, the MR-2 Spyder, and the Echo. The attempt could not have been more heavy-handed. It was like the University of Kansas marching band trying to play hip-hop. The target customers could not have been less interested. Toyota cancelled all three within five years and resolved never to create any new model without asking customers first.

It's not as if Toyota didn't know how to design a new model to meet customers' desires. Some years before, in 1986, the company sent a team of designers and engineers to southern California to "live the good life." The expense accounts, so it is said, were so astronomical as to cause near-fainting spells back at the home office. Toyota had decided to make a giant leap and get into the elite-car business alongside Jaguar, BMW, Mercedes, and Cadillac. It realized that it knew virtually nothing about the typical buyers of these special cars, and so it sent the team to live among these people and see firsthand what they cared about.

What they cared about was luxury—the feeling, aromas, and ambience of luxury. These customers could buy any car they wanted. Their choice hinged around service and image: How will I look driving this machine? After living among elite buyers for a year, and after designing a car that would appeal to such people, Toyota unwrapped its first independent brand—the Lexus. Even the name, highly researched, suggested specialness.

It was an instant hit. Twenty years later, *Business Week* cited Lexus as among the top 10 "customer service elite" brands in the world. Now *that* is what people mean by listening to your customers—hangovers and all.

Chapter Five

Toyota's Impact on Society and the Industrial World

People who read about the history of the Toyota Motor Corporation often stop at about this point and wonder to themselves: Since Toyota is so obviously successful in all that it does—since it seems to have all of the production challenges figured out—why don't other manufacturers simply emulate it? In fact, why don't all companies, from tax preparers to skyscraper builders, copy the Toyota way of doing things?

The answer, like all things to do with Toyota, is complex. A few pages from now I'll examine in some detail the seven elements that distinguish Toyota from all other companies.

Before that, however, it would be good to consider the context of Toyota's ongoing achievement. Toyota is best considered against two differing backgrounds: the culture from which the company grew and the common qualities that all world-class achievers share.

First and above all, it is a *Japanese* company. Japan's culture is unique in world history, which is why I spent some time in the beginning with an historical overview. Saab got its start, of course, as a Swedish car, but it does not find its central identity in Nordic culture. Peugeot is made by French manufacturers, but it is more of a world car than a French car. Toyota, alone among carmakers, is entirely Japanese. The culture from which Toyota grew colors the company the way chlorophyll colors grass. This is also true to some extent about all companies that were originally Japanese, such as Nissan and Sony. Toyota alone, however, fully identifies its processes—and its success—with its Japanese roots.

The second useful background to consider is larger. Toyota may also be best understood against a global background of magnificent achievement. What all great enterprises have in common is that they are conceived in courage.

What great adventurers and explorers and business innovators do is launch out into the future with few guidelines and no charts, because they are heading into unexplored territory. The truly great ones understand that once the course is set, there is no turning back. We succeed or fail. There is no middle ground. Captain James Cook, Ferdinand Magellan, Lewis and Clark, Captain Robert FitzRoy, Christopher Columbus—and a hundred more—are among history's giants because they stepped out into the unknown with minimal supplies and a powerful self-confidence that they could meet whatever challenges came their way.

What Toyota has done in a business enterprise, others have done on a more personal basis. But they all have that common bond of courage.

In 1912, Sir Ernest Shackleton and a crew of 27 sailed to the frozen seas of the Antarctic Ocean and got hopelessly stuck in the ice. That is, their ship, the *Endurance,* was hopeless. It was lost. The men and their leader were full of hope. Their one chance was to hike across the icebound wasteland and pray that they were headed in the right direction. One mistake and they would all die.

Shackleton gave a now-famous talk to the crew before they set off. Get rid of everything, he said, that will prevent us from reaching our destination quickly. Tents, extra provisions, extra water, coins, books, candles, extra blankets—all were tossed into the snow. If they tried to carry safety backups, they would founder on the glaciers and die. Go lean, and they might live. They trekked for days and reached the safety of a whaling village. They lived, because they discarded their backup provisions.

In 1969, the United States landed a spacecraft on the moon. The world collectively held its breath several days later as the astronauts ignited the engines for lift-off. They had only one chance. They had no safety backups—to carry extra supplies would have made the craft too heavy to make the journey. And so they went lean, giving themselves one chance to come back to earth. It worked.

The principle is sound: If you carry too many backup provisions, the very things you hoped would help you succeed would weigh you down and doom you to failure.

In the long recovery period in Japan after World War II, Toyota executives knew they had only one chance to make automobiles successfully: They must go lean. The Americans and Europeans were in a sense recovering also from the war, but they had vast reservoirs of wealth and energy compared to Japan. Toyota's grand act of courage was braced by desperation—there was no other option. It had few resources of its own, limited capital, no experience, and no market for its products. It was already as lean as fence posts. Its only hope of staying alive was to turn leanness into an advantage.

Out of necessity, Toyota created the Toyota Production System, known today in short as TPS. Often it is called "lean production." It was built on two foundations: just-in-time and *jidoka,* the (at the time) contrarian notion that even the lowliest worker could stop the line. *Jidoka,* in isolating defects rather than passing them downstream, is the only method that ensures quality in the line from start to finish.

The strength of those two concepts enabled Toyota to invent the first inexpensive, high-quality car.

TPS AND THE QUEST FOR QUALITY

The essential challenge in mass-producing and selling any car for lower-middle-class and middle-class buyers is to give it a low price while maintaining high quality. Manufacturers can meet that challenge by producing small cars and creating new categories called compacts, subcompacts, and even miniatures. The second challenge, then, is to convince the market that it really does want small cars.

The task was relatively easy in Europe, with its dense cities and narrow, winding roads that were frequently blocked by sheep or cows. London, Milan, Berlin, and Paris had essentially no parking. Apartment buildings are built right up to the street, and public space for any activity is rare.

In America, the challenge was on a different scale altogether. Cities like Boston and Philadelphia were similar to cities in Europe, with their tight parking restrictions and narrow roads built on original cow paths. But cities like Omaha and Austin, Cleveland and Minneapolis were wide open. Americans were used to having acres of parking and big cars that drank big gallons of gas. When gas supplies started to dwindle and prices started to rise in the mid-1970s, even the Americans turned their attention toward smaller, well-built automobiles.

The elite cars had their market. The cheap road-beaters were fine for college kids and grannies on a fixed income. Everybody else wanted a good ride—cheap. They had to look long and hard to find something. They flirted for a time with Italy's Fiat and with France's Peugeot and Renault. These cars were certainly small enough to park in Boston's overcrowded Copley Square or near Philly's Independence Hall. But they were thin and tended not to stand up to an American winter.

In 1954, Eiji Toyoda believed he could deliver exactly the right car at exactly the right price. But, like everything else the company had done to this point, it wouldn't be easy.

What Would You Do?

Making good decisions is more art than science. Experts have developed formulas for helping us assign numbers to choices. Just add up the numbers, they say, and making good decisions seems more like a mathematical certainty than the random spin of the universe's roulette wheel. Perhaps. Political leaders and business executives know in their hearts, however, that a good decision is more often the result of intuition and good luck than anything else.

Here's an example.

Let's say you are the CEO of Chrysler Corporation, and the year is 1997. You are happy. Everything, finally, is going your way. For years you have suffered because of the way Toyota has beat you and your company over the head with all this palaver about "just in time" and "lean production" and blah blah blah.

But wait a minute—why are you happy? Because you have started to out-Toyota Toyota and it has started to get nervous. An American car company is finally getting it right!

It all started with your predecessor, Lee Iacocca. He came over from Ford and brought Chrysler back from the brink of disaster in the early 1980s. He did it in several ways. First, he borrowed money from the American government (meaning, of course, American taxpayers) with his personal promise to pay it back with interest. He did this on television, speaking directly to the American people. He was utterly convincing, and he made it work.

Second, he and his engineers developed the famous K-Car. It consisted of roughly a K-shaped undercarriage that formed the literal foundation for all the cars that Chrysler made in the decade to follow.

Third, and perhaps most important, he created a new culture at Chrysler—a culture of excellence that he learned from Toyota. Part of the excellence of the new culture was the power he gave to hands-on engineers.

Fourth, he brought in outstanding managers to take his place. They in turn set up work teams (again, like Toyota) with people who were directly responsible for the electrical systems, body and chassis, power train, and manufacturing systems. Things started to hum. And Americans started to buy Chrysler again.

The K-Car paved the way for the famous LH series that included the Dodge Intrepid, the Concorde, the Neon, the powerhouse Jeep Grand Cherokee, and the PT Cruiser. The Americans were beating the Japanese at their own game! For most of the 1990s, Chrysler was flying high. The new culture of excellence was working; engineers were concentrating on quality again. It was class production, not mass production. Customers flocked into the dealerships. Toyota started to lose sales to American cars—unthinkable for a generation or more of Toyota and Honda and Nissan fans. Chrysler was soon recognized as the maker of the world's most profitable cars.

Then something important happened (you knew it would).

Daimler, the famous German maker of Mercedes-Benz automobiles, made Chrysler an offer it couldn't ignore: $36 billion. (Around $51 billion in today's dollars.) And you, the CEO, now have a decision to make. Do you refuse the offer and place all your bets on an American car company winning against the Japanese? Or do you take the offer and put all the might of Daimler cash reserves and the magnificent Mercedes-Benz brand on your side?

What would you do?

What Did Chrysler Do?

It sold out to Daimler. It simply couldn't resist the lure of all that money and one of the biggest names in the automotive world. The renewed energy and excitement the Chrysler people had been enjoying up to this point went right up in smoke, along with most of the senior engineers and managers.

It was a disaster from the start. German culture clashed with American culture, and everybody lost. The Germans demanded draconian cost cutting and the sharing of the technology that Iacocca and his followers had worked so hard to create.

By 2000, Chrysler was teetering on the brink of bankruptcy again. By the end of 2006, Chrysler reported losses of $1.5 billion. In February 2007, it laid off 13,000 people. Several months later, Daimler cut its losses and sold Chrysler for a loss to another company.

For one thing, government ministers believed they were obliged to undergird Japan's nascent automotive industry and took strong steps to make it happen. They banned outright the importation of foreign cars that arrived ready to drive, while allowing the imports to be assembled in Japan by indigenous workers.

They also looked closely at Germany, which had been nearly as devastated as Japan was 10 years before. Germany was making a surprising comeback—like Japan, Germany had strong American business support—and an important part of the recovery was the popularity of the Volkswagen, which in German means "people's car" or "vehicle of the people."

Ferdinand Porsche had designed this beetle-like little car 20 years earlier, and it had proved to be massively popular. It was cheap, sporty, and peppy and had a miraculous air-cooled engine—the ideal car for singles or young couples who lived in northern cities. Now the VW was making inroads in the United States, and Japan was taking notice.

Eiji Toyoda had already noticed. He kept crunching the numbers, trying to make them work for him. At the time, a VW in Germany cost $890. A Toyota Crown in Japan cost $2,300. The Crown was an intermediate, not a mini; maybe he could make a smaller car at a price within range of the VW.

THE BIRTH OF THE CORONA

Or maybe not. His government and his own company president, Taizo Ishida, were applying pressure on him relentlessly to get something into production that could rival VW and the new model that Nissan was bragging about. There was no time for a ground-up redesign; he would have to cannibalize the models that were already in production. He took the Crown's drive train, sliced off inches from the front and back and sides, and started work on a single-construction body. Along the way, somebody thought up a new name for the car: Corona, a small crown.

The government, for once, helped. It subsidized Toyota's vendors with low-interest loans, enabling them to enter the fight with modernized equipment capable of punching out the smaller, lighter parts needed for the Corona.

In 1957, the Corona burst onto the scene and immediately grabbed the attention of industry journalists and an intrigued public. Toyota was a strong name in Japan. People jumped at the chance to own this new compact and drove it around with the pleasure that being on the cutting edge brings.

But the party was over almost before it got started. Corona customers stormed back into the dealerships with a whole litany of disasters: not enough power, too heavy, too expensive on fuel, and it keeps breaking down. Anything else? Well, now that you mention it, we don't need a weather report to tell us when it rains because the thing leaks like a paper umbrella.

It was a disaster, but it could be fixed. Toyota was always trustworthy, people knew, and would make it right. Instead of looking for shelter, Eiji Toyoda did what by now everyone had come to expect of anyone named Toyoda: He did the opposite thing. He bought a huge piece of land in Koromo, in the Honshu district, alongside the Yahagi River, about 150 miles southwest of Tokyo. The area had once been the home of a medieval castle; it would become a fortress again for the Toyota Motor Company. In 1959, the town officially changed its name to Toyota City.

In an attempt to gain a toehold in the U.S. market, that same year Toyota shipped 2,000 Crowns to a weed-infested lot in Hollywood, where they languished like a child star nobody wanted to see anymore. The company sent over a new model, called the Tiara, and a pickup truck, but nobody wanted them, either. It was starting to get embarrassing. One bright spot was the Land Cruiser, a beefy four-wheeler that Toyota had built for use in the Korean War. It caught on, enough to keep the dealership alive.

Europe was getting in on the act, as well, with the VW beetle garnering droves of enthusiasts. By now the Big Three in Detroit had smelled the coffee and had started to showcase their own compact versions. The future for Toyota in America looked grim. How grim? In 1960, Toyota sold only 316 cars. Eiji Toyoda came over himself to fire half of his American workforce.

Meanwhile, back in Japan, Nissan was eating Toyota's lunch. Nissan's sleek sedans, with their styling honed to Japanese tastes and their steadily increasing performance, made a hash out of Eiji's plans to dominate the domestic market. Toyota owned the domestic truck market, as it always had, thanks to government contracts, but Nissan owned the domestic car market.

When the news wasn't bad, it was worse. Quality in the new plant was suffering. The new cars the workers were churning out looked good, thanks to the just-in-time performance of suppliers, but did not drive well. Too many cars needed repairing after production. Customers started to complain loudly to the company and to each other. Disaster loomed just ahead.

It was time to call in the one man who could possibly turn all this around: W. Edwards Deming.

THE DEMING CYCLE WORKS IN TOTAL . . . OR NOT AT ALL

The contributions of the quality guru Deming to the improvement of Toyota are all-encompassing. (We introduced you to Deming, recall, in chapter three.) His ideas run the gamut from hiring people with exactly the right attitude to broadening "customer" to include the guy working just downstream from you. When Toyota enfolded Deming's business philosophies into its own just-in-time network, the result was an organic reworking of the company's infrastructure to change the very nature of the way a manufacturer produces things.

In other words, Toyota appropriated the whole package.

Most companies pick and choose what they like about Dr. Deming's principles and ignore the rest, like students ignoring broccoli in the cafeteria line and loading up on dessert.

Deming's ideas don't work that way. You take them all, or you take nothing.

Deming's improvement cycle is specific: Plan-Do-Check-Act (PDCA). In other words, after planning and adding a certain value to a product, you check your work for quality while it's still on the line and act to fix it if there is a defect. That was Deming's vision.

Most companies are happy to do only the first two elements in the cycle. Plan and Do. "There," you can hear them saying, "we've followed the Deming Cycle for the most part. Let's go get coffee."

Toyota, virtually alone among manufacturers, even Japanese ones, follows every letter of Deming's principles. It's one of the reasons Toyota is alone at the top of automobile manufacturers.

Deming, together with TPS, solved Toyota's quality problems, allowing the Corona to gain a toehold in the United States and to pave the way for the even more successful Corolla. Toyota was on its way to becoming a world-class car company.

Let's take a closer look at the systems, ideas, and processes that helped ensure its success.

Many good American companies have respect for individuals, and practice *kaizen* and other TPS tools. But what is important is having all the elements together as a system. It must be practiced every day in a very consistent manner—not in spurts—in a concrete way on the shop floor.

—Fujio Cho, Board of Directors, Toyota Motor Corporation

TOYOTA PRODUCTION SYSTEM

That TPS is called a *system* is somewhat misleading, especially if one considers Western car-making methods as a prototypical system.

Traditionally, the West systematizes the manufacturing of vehicles by building workstations to perform one activity and by training workers to perform one or two limited tasks. Supervisors are looking not for creativity but for strict adherence to procedures outlined in the relevant manual. Workers are paid based on how well and efficiently they follow the rules. The system is clear: Executives write the rules, supervisors administer them, and workers follow them.

This system is ideal when demand is strong and the larger economy is sound.

Let's say that you are hired and trained to make a D-ring metal gasket and an S-wave cotter pin to hold the brake-pad assembly in place. You shape the gasket and pin, then put them in place as each axle with its brake assembly rolls by your station.

During lunch one day, you think of a clever way to make the gasket and pin in one pressing rather than two. It would involve reconfiguring one metal stamping machine with a new die and possibly shutting down the line for up to three hours. But it will save several hundred man-hours over a year's time and possibly decrease the per-unit cost of vehicles by as much as $18. Do you take the idea to your supervisor?

No.

That kind of bottom-up innovation is seldom encouraged in Western plants. Once the system is in place, they press the GO button, and it runs. Western supervisors tend not to trust their workers to work every minute of the day with the company's interests—rather than their own—uppermost in their minds. That slight reservation—that tendency not to trust the "common good" ethos among workers—may be the single most important factor that has kept Western carmakers mired in the ways of the past and that has impelled Toyota to achieve more sales and a better quality image than Detroit's Big Three. Toyota trusts its workers; Western supervisors trust the system over the people, and they may be right to do so. Working together for the greater good of the company is not a cornerstone of Western culture. Westerners see themselves as individuals first and as team members second.

The big exception, of course, is at any Toyota plant in the United States from Texas to Kentucky. American workers new to Toyota quickly learn that they will succeed individually only to the degree that they work with a *kaizen* attitude for the company. Thinking up ways to improve your work while on a lunch break is the rule, and everyone buys into it. Toyota looks for that standard right from the start in the hiring process. One is free not to agree with the company-and-customer-first emphasis on teamwork, just as one is free to look for employment elsewhere.

The key to Toyota's success is precisely that kind of lunch-hour thinking. Each worker, without exception, is expected to do everything possible to improve the process continually. At Toyota, a worker with an idea to save $18 per unit would be highly praised. The worker, while inwardly happy, would be outwardly modest about accepting such praise for merely doing his or her job.

Toyota's Famous Five Whys in Action

Let's say you are a junior executive at Toyota's Kentucky plant, and you have an idea for a new body style for Toyota's midsize pickup truck for the Idaho potato-farmer market. Your idea has gone up the channels, and you have been invited to come to Japan to present your idea.

At a minimum, expect the Five Whys.

Executive:	Why are you recommending a new body style for potato farmers?
You:	Because the current style does not fit their needs.
Executive:	Why does it not fit their needs?
You:	Because it opens from the rear. Potato farmers need a truck with a body that's lower on one side and can be open and shut like a tailgate.
Executive:	Why do they need a side opening rather than a tailgate?
You:	Because the front buckets on the tractors are too wide to fit the rear opening.
Executive:	Why don't they use narrower buckets on the tractors?
You:	Because potatoes are perishable in the weather and need to be loaded as quickly as possible.
Executive:	Why can't the tractors lift over the sides as they are now?
You:	Because they load directly from the fields, where the tractors work from the furrows, with the trucks high above them. Too high for safety.

Try the Five Whys yourself on a problem and see if it works.

Toyota, unlike industries in other cultures, trains its 250,000 workers worldwide to see procedural manuals as guidelines, not commandments set in stone. New hires frequently testify that they are curious about why Toyota spurns specific instructions for doing a job, preferring instead (within obvious limits based on experience) to let workers discover the best ways of doing a task—and then to discover even better ways of doing it.

The thinking is simple: No executives or supervisors can possibly be expected to come up with the myriad details of minuscule improvements that line workers can. No procedural manual can by definition be current if it took more than a few hours to write it.

Dr. Deming taught his Japanese disciples in the early days that principles should be firm and far-reaching but that methods are subject to constant improvement. What works today will likely not work tomorrow, Deming said, so improve, improve, improve. Dr. Deming is still revered in Toyota's culture; his sayings and principles are still admired. Deming often said in later life that he was somewhat surprised that Western manufacturers were reluctant to embrace what his Japanese students saw as wisdom. The worldwide success of *kaizen* underscores that he was right to be surprised; *kaizen* is still largely ignored or considered too difficult or too expensive by many leading companies.

How, then, does Toyota maintain its culture of Japanese values across a worldwide spectrum of models and customers and workers? The answer is breathtakingly simple (in the way that Einstein's $E = MC^2$ formula is simple), so let's take a look at it.

SEVEN ATTRIBUTES THAT DISTINGUISH TOYOTA FROM ALL OTHER CARMAKERS

Professional poker players say that the simplest version of poker, known as Texas Hold-'Em, takes 10 minutes to learn and a lifetime to master. What they often mean by that is that the rules are easy, but, since the game is played in the context of human nature, success takes deep wisdom.

One could say that about Toyota, as well. What the company does to stand out from all others is simple, really. There is no magic involved. Toyota's culture is transparent to all who care to examine it. The key is that its simplicity is based on an understanding of human nature, and human nature is still the longest-running study of humankind.

Human beings are imperfect. They make mistakes. They tend to be motivated by self-interest. When left unsupervised, they sometimes cut corners. When oversupervised, they tend to resent it and find small ways for revenge. They are capable of heroic action. They can be loyal and disloyal. They can be reliable and unreliable. And so on. (You can fill in the rest yourself, as human nature is infinitely complex.)

So how does a company give itself the best chance to succeed, other than creating a workplace filled with robots rather than humans?

Here are some of the main ways Toyota does it.

Understand That All Human Beings Have Good Reasons to Be Humble

Japanese culture, for thousands of years, has promoted the virtues of humility. Arrogance in any context is unwelcome. This understanding is certainly not unique to Japan. Many cultures and many religions have suggested that humility is fundamental to spiritual growth. In Japan, however, humility is expected. To be disrespectful of others is to disgrace one's family and one's name.

Toyota's executives take public transportation to work and fly coach. They do not have designated parking spaces near the front door. They do not flaunt their status in any way. They are not paid as well as American car executives and are known once in a while to get shop dirt on a crisp white shirt. It would be unthinkable for a vice president to be chauffeured to work while the president shows up in a carpool.

Toyota's highest executives, of course, are far better paid than line workers. They carry the burdens of management and responsibility far more than line workers do and tend to work much longer hours. That said, they are paid less than executives in similar positions in other companies. In 2006, for example, while Nissan's top executives averaged about $2 million, Toyota's leaders earned around one-fourth of that. In further contrast, top Detroit executives earned in the tens of millions—for much less impressive performance.

Such humility is not merely for show. It is recognition that great enterprises require the efforts of everyone involved. Who is needed more—the executive who writes a report in the afternoon or the machinist who discovers a faster way to install fresh drill bits? The answer is that both are needed equally. For an executive to think that he or she is more important than the line worker is ultimately to "lose face." In Japanese culture, it is difficult to recover from losing face.

Consider the Parking Lot

If you are looking for an interesting "chalk circle" experiment (where you stand in place and simply observe), go early to the parking lot of any large American company, find a safe, inconspicuous spot to stand or sit, and watch what happens.

No matter how early you are, some people will already be there. In Canada, they call them "keeners," people who are keen to advance their careers. They will park near the door. But not too near it, because really near the door will be several spaces appropriately reserved for people with disabilities. Even closer to the door will be spaces marked with the name of the president and the names of several vice presidents. There might even be one grand space marked "Employee of the Month."

As eight o'clock nears, the lot will start filling up. Most people will park as near the door as they can get legally. Some with expensive cars will park farther away in hopes of avoiding dents from thoughtless drivers of obviously cheaper cars.

As the starting hour chimes, most people will be wending their way into the building and noticing that—yet again—the president and one or two vice presidents have yet to show up. Now these executives may be having a breakfast meeting with an important client. But what occurs to most employees dragging themselves past the prime parking slots is that the honchos have not yet managed to get to work.

What are some implications of this thinking? If you were the president, would you really want people to walk past your spot and think evil thoughts of you? Would you care? If you were the president, what would your parking lot policy be?

At Toyota, there are no reserved parking spaces. Is this a good or a poor policy, and why?

Humility as a way of working does several good things for people. It promotes respect across the workspace. It tends to keep gossip down and support for others up. It mitigates the tendency of most people to think that what they are doing is the most important thing to be doing at the time. It underscores the value of listening to others. And humility emphasizes the long view. We might be world leaders today, but tomorrow can bring a different story. Therefore, it's best to be gracious in success and quietly determined in failure, for both will surely come our way.

Perhaps the best reason of all for humility is that it is essential for *kaizen*. A worker who thinks he is right all the time is placing himself as an obstacle to *kaizen*. Humility supports the thinking of someone who says I—even I!—could possibly do this job better. The opposite of humility is an unacceptable arrogance that hinders achievement.

Some say this is precisely the point where Toyota's *Japaneseness* separates the company irrevocably from all others, especially all Western manufacturers. This is the point where Western culture stops, and it has to do with a willingness not only to admit error but to feel genuine inward regret that one has made an error and is in need of correction.

The Japanese word is *hansei*. It is the one concept that Toyota finds Western emulators are unwilling to embrace. In fact, there is no comparable word in Western languages. In essence, it means "to look inward," to "reflect" on what one has done wrong. In practice, it means to react in a particular way to criticism—to embrace the criticism and feel sorry that one has forced one's superiors to offer corrective advice.

This is where Americans, especially, draw the line. We are loath to admit culpability for anything, much less to feel bad about it or to regret that a supervisor had to correct us about it. The typical American response to criticism is to withdraw and sulk like Achilles in his tent or to push back against the one who is criticizing.

Unfortunately for Western workers trying to implement continuous improvement, *hansei* is central to *kaizen*. We will not feel a proper sense of urgency to correct a defect, the thinking goes, unless we are sorry for it. Our sorrow is necessary for our *kaizen* attitude of total correction.

I was at a professional conference recently in which an American speaker unwittingly gave certitude to this point.

"I asked my biggest client," he said, "to give me feedback on the service I was giving him." The speaker expected fulsome praise, as the client had been with him for a number of years to the exclusion of all other vendors.

"Since you asked," the client offered, "you are a pure pain to work with. You are arrogant, you don't listen to me, you come in to my office with a chip on your shoulder and lecture me on what I have to do to make you happy. I would fire you instantly, except I can't find anyone with prices as good as yours. The moment I do, you're out of here. But thanks for asking."

The speaker, of course, milked the moment while the audience laughed. "My response," he said, "was to tell the client how wrong he was."

This notion of *hansei* goes to the heart of one's ability to accept criticism. Japanese style is to offer criticism routinely, as a way of showing respect for the fact that the person receiving the criticism can—and wants to—improve. Praise is rare in older Japanese culture. Why should one be praised for doing what is good and honorable? It is the responsibility of superiors to help workers improve—by offering criticism and having it received humbly and gratefully.

The only organization in the West that I can think of that comes anywhere close to the concept of *hansei* is the United States Marine Corps. In boot camp, a recruit is systematically and harshly reduced to his essence: a living, breathing human being, or at least a facsimile of one. His head is shaved. He is stripped naked of all previous associations and given a uniform in an unusual shade of green. The drill instructors then go out of their way for many weeks to show the recruit how woefully short of the standard he comes. The recruit finds himself scrubbing the restrooms (called "latrines") with toothbrushes—not to get the place clean so much as to demonstrate to the recruit how far he has to go. His body is pummeled into shape. He is taught to love and care for his rifle, to recite the Marine Corps hymn and the Rifleman's Creed on demand, to respect all superiors (to a recruit, that's anything that moves), and to obey all lawful orders instantly.

If he or she is careful and humble and works hard, the recruit is one fine day declared to be a United States Marine, someone who never again is unsure about his or her identity. Only when one is sure of one's identity is humility a genuine sign of great strength.

Other than the Marines, there is no precedent for such thoughtful humility in Western culture. It is as foreign to the Western mind as eating poisonous blowfish—raw.

Invest in the Future

Toyota is fierce in planning for tomorrow. Given its success over other carmakers, it can afford to be. Where Detroit's Big Three are burdened by union actions and pensions of people long retired, Toyota spends more than $10 million a day in research and development.

Perhaps the best example of how Toyota constantly thinks about the future is in the classic battle between Ford's Taurus and Toyota's Camry, with America as the battleground.

When Ford executives looked to the future in the early 1980s, the picture was bleak. They were slipping down the slope of declining sales into failure. Ford! America's car company! The carmaker that defined the car culture for America at the turn of the twentieth century was in danger of bankruptcy. Henry Ford would doubtless have preferred death to seeing such an unthinkable thing as the Ford Motor Company coming to ruin.

America was trying to recover from the gas shortages of 1973 and 1980, and part of the answer was the Corolla—perky and miserly on gas, it drove past every car mechanic's shop in town.

Ford engineers went to work and came up with the Taurus, one of the best-designed and best-functioning cars Ford ever built. It looked kind of like a jellybean, but engineers liked it, and so did drivers. Launched in 1985, Taurus saved Ford. Soccer moms and college students, librarians, and just-promoted vice presidents flocked to the showrooms and drove off with a Taurus. Suddenly there were Tauruses everywhere, from Main Street to Wall Street. Seven years of great sales knocked Honda's powerhouse Accord out of the top spot. In 1992, Ford sold nearly half a million Tauruses. Drivers, for their part, were glad to be driving an American car again. Ford execs put on sunglasses and envisioned a bright future. They were kicking Corolla around the track and enjoying every lap.

But the future got dark again for Ford. Toyota decided that Corolla was what it was; it had a better answer waiting in the wings.

Toyota took a long hard look at Camry and knew a winner when it saw one. Now was the time to reconfigure the Camry model. Sedate and solid when it first came out, Camry was nobody's idea of a plush ride. But it was a good value, like all Toyotas, and demonstrated an unusual desire to run forever. If "plain vanilla" was continually linked with Camry, nobody at Toyota minded. The vanilla bean is, after all, among the rarest and most delicious spices in the world.

When the Georgetown, Kentucky, plant opened, in 1988, Toyota got serious about the Camry. It wanted something that would kill and deliver last rites to the Taurus, and Camry was elected.

The divine wind was blowing in a fair direction once more. The Lexus had opened to rave reviews in the early 1990s, and what Toyota had learned in producing it was worth billions in market share. The company would do for the Camry what it had just done for Lexus.

It restyled the Camry onto a Lexus base. It was like touching gold. The Taurus was worrisome, of course, but Toyota, which now was a serious player in the luxury market, could envision millions of subluxury customers flocking to a working-man's Lexus. So it spared no expense and no effort. The 1992 Camry burst onto the scene loaded for bear: passenger air bags, an aluminum engine for performance, a sexy new design, and rich designer colors. The interior was soft and elegant. Knobs, buttons, levers were just where you wanted them. Seats were roomy and comfortable. The ride was close to what many people (who had never been in one) imagined a Rolls-Royce delivered.

It was overkill—the best midsize sedan ever constructed on the planet. And what it overkilled was Taurus.

Ford execs, hunkered down in Detroit, fought back. They pushed Taurus into fleet and rental car sales with sharply discounted prices just to keep the line moving while they rethought the whole package. (One former Ford engineer said he was dismayed when they took the Camry apart—it really was too good to be true.)

Ford tried to do to the Taurus what Toyota had done to the Camry, but in the end it failed. There was no consensus from the top, and the line workers had no motivation to think up any ways to improve the product. Everyone at Ford just seemed tired of Taurus. The new version in 1996 was greeted with catcalls from the automotive press. Buyers had too many alternatives now, far more than at the time of the Taurus's first introduction. Even people who wanted to "buy American" could see no reason not to buy a Camry, which now was built from the tires up in the United States. Ford stopped producing the Taurus in 2006. It was the one brand in two generations that had even a chance to beat Toyota at its own game; the people involved had realized that they couldn't play the game at all. Ford gave it all the money and all the hard work it had, but in the end it understood that Toyota *begins* with money and hard work and turns up the heat from there.

To some of the world's car customers, Camry is still considered a luxury car.

Immerse Everyone in the Corporate Culture

In 2001, Toyota announced its new global training center to the world: the Toyota Institute. Like France's Academie Française, which exists to preserve the glories of the French language, Toyota Institute's mission is to imbue key workers from around the world with a clear sense of where Toyota comes from and what its unique identity is. Toyota is a brand that has come to mean a great deal to millions of car buyers in almost every country. The Institute exists to make sure that the people involved in making Toyota vehicles never forget who they are.

It starts with an unwavering respect for other people. Blame, as Kiichiro Toyoda said so long ago, is the essence of waste, yet assigning blame for a mistake is characteristic of so many Western industries. Casting blame is also disrespectful. The essential culture of Toyota is that workers are the company. The solutions and advances that have made Toyota a great brand will continue to come from the people who make the vehicles with their own hands.

Toyota culture is built on a three-brick foundation that will not wobble: process, people, and technology. Let's examine all three, beginning with the most important.

1. *Process Is Outcome.* The correct process leads inevitably to the outcome you want. Toyota started with this and has stayed with it for nearly one hundred years. Process well conceived and continually improved is fundamental to success the way good grapes are fundamental to good wine.

Perhaps the value of process can best be appreciated in its absence and illustrated by a true story.

My advertising agency colleagues and I were entertaining some clients at a famous celebrity-owned restaurant. We were a noisy but well-behaved group of eight, and having a great time. Nearby, a bus boy carrying a tray of cleared plates dropped one accidentally. The plate shattered on the floor. The worker picked up the pieces but left a spray of tomato sauce on the tiles. I was about to make a point concerning our latest campaign to the group when I noticed an elderly woman walking inexorably into the spill. Before I could yell to warn her, she slipped and landed hard on her back on the floor. No one in the restaurant moved, including the staff.

I rushed over to her and was joined, fortunately, by an off-duty nurse. The nurse determined after a time that the woman could stand up, and we helped her to her feet and back to her table. I went back to my group, assuming that the restaurant staff would deal with the spill. They did not.

A few minutes later, another patron was unknowingly walking into the spill, and I got to him just in time to avert another disaster. I found the manager and suggested to him that it was not my job to guard the spill. He said they were terribly busy but put a chair over the spill to keep people away. It wasn't enough.

You might not believe me, but 10 minutes later a waitress managed to walk close enough to the spill to slip and scatter several plates full of food in all directions.

My colleagues and I left the staff to its own devices and went off in search of a more congenial establishment.

In discussing the incident later, we decided that the restaurant did not have a *process* for dealing with such an emergency. No one felt it was his or her job to stop performing the essential functions of a restaurant—preparing and serving food and beverages—in order to deal with something so mundane and non-income-producing as a spill on the floor. I had an image in my mind that in an hour's time there would be a dozen patrons flat on their backs around the spill while the staff blithely brought dinners to tables.

Every manufacturing activity requires a process. The process should include a means for continuous improvement, as well as a way to make sure that defects do not recur. In other words, *kaizen* tends to look upstream anytime a problem presents itself.

If one were to arrange the way Toyota solves problems, it might look like this:

Discover a problem	PLAN
Study the problem or chalk circle it	
Verbalize the actual problem	DO
Identify the physical location of the cause of the problem	
Ask the Five Whys	
Develop a long-term solution	
Evaluate the solution	CHECK
Implement the solution by standardizing the improvement	ACT

You may notice that this system is the Deming Wheel in practice. In the case of the restaurant scenario, let's play this out. The problem and its location are obvious. (In any complex manufacturing process, these would not be obvious.) So let's pick up the process with the Five Whys.

- Why was the spill not cleaned up?
  No one is available for cleanup duty during the busy dinner hour.

- Why is no one available?
  Because the manager has not assigned anyone to the job.

- Why has he not assigned anyone?
  Because every staff member is needed to keep the plates moving quickly from kitchen to table.

- Why is that important?
  Because keeping patrons happy with hot food, brought to everyone at the tables at the same time, is the manager's top priority, not their safety.

- Why is patron safety not his top priority?
  Because the owner does not include patron safety in evaluating the manager's effectiveness.

Now we know that any long-term solution must include patron safety in measuring the manager's effectiveness. We might also interview the staff for their ideas about spills and other defects that might threaten patron safety. Then we would rewrite the procedural manual and train the manager and all staff in the importance of patron safety above all other considerations. Patrons will not sue us if their lasagna is only tepid and not hot. They will sue us if granny breaks an arm while slipping on a spill.

One final note: Improvement is not long-lasting unless we standard-ize it. Memories are short. Personnel come and go. An improved process as part of standard procedure lasts until the next improved standard procedure.

2. *People Have Ideas; Machines Do Not.* The second brick upon which Toyota's culture is built is a recognition of the unique value of people. Toyota hires for life. Except for some kind of dereliction, if you leave it will be your choice.

From the start, Toyota has made it public that people matter. They are not discardable, and they are not interchangeable. Each person is unique, with unique ideas and unique perceptions. Further, they can be trained and rewarded to come up with improvements if the organization wishes to invest in such training.

Most organizations do not wish to invest in the longevity of work-ers. They tend to see people as interchangeable. But in turnover there is extreme waste. Turnover is the number one complaint of many U.S. orga-nizations. Toyota decided decades ago that it can reduce such waste to a minimum by hiring for life.

As yet, machines do not think, but people do. Toyota rewards thinking.

3. *Technology Lives in Ideas.* Toyota's third cultural brick, technology, is last because, while important, it is not as important as the first two. Technology resides not in wires or electrons but in ideas.

The moveable assembly line, just-in-time delivery, lean production—all these and hundreds of practices like them were based on innovative ideas, not innovative technology. Technology that does not serve improve-ment is of no value. Further, technology can be duplicated by one's com-petition. It was only a matter of months after Henry Ford introduced the moveable assembly line that every other carmaker had one, as well.

Moving from Gutenberg's one-ton metal printing press to today's three-pound laptops and one-pound laser printers took giant leaps of technology—but each of those leaps was driven by ideas fueled by inno-vation, and not the reverse.

Technology is vital, certainly, to compete in the twenty-first century. But Toyota continues to invest most heavily where it always has—in people and their ideas.

Remove Waste from the Process, No Matter How Small

All Toyota plants have achieved something that most other manufac-turing operations can only dream of: near-zero waste of raw materials at the end of the process. Toyota still throws out paper and plastic waste for recycling. Yet, for all the tons of raw materials it brings into the plants, virtually none leaves except as part of the vehicles or as scraps to be recycled into the next batch of raw materials. Nothing metallic goes to waste.

Even more important, a worker's time does not go to waste. In September 1990, *The Economist* magazine, based in London, reported a lengthy comparison of the different manufacturing styles of General Motors and Toyota.

The article started with GM's assembly plant in Framingham, Massachusetts, where the reporter found that "several weeks' worth of parts are piled beside a cluttered assembly line. The workflow is erratic. Some people are rushing around; others have time to read a newspaper. At the end of the line, cars riddled with faults wait to be repaired. The dispirited workers have been laid off half a dozen times in the past ten years."

The contrast could not have been more stunning. Touring Toyota's Takaoka plant in Nagoya, the reporter describes the clean aisles as "deliberately narrow. There is no room to store inventories; parts are delivered on a *just-in-time* basis. All the employees work at about the same pace. If a problem arises, they can pull cords to stop the production line at any time. They have jobs for life. Almost every Toyota is driven directly away for delivery without needing repair."

The reporter noted that the Framingham plant closed a short time later.

Promote Cleanliness as the Father of Profitability

Visitors to any Toyota plant often remark that the place rivals a hospital for cleanliness. In Toyota's culture, clutter is distracting. If a worker is thinking about what to do with trash, he or she is not thinking about how to make the process better. Therefore, clutter has to go.

Suppliers are trained to deliver components in packaging that is returnable and reusable. There are bins for a variety of materials to be recycled. Around the world, Toyota plants add nothing to landfills.

Toyota devotes such attention to managing and reducing waste for three reasons. First, it is good business practice. It saves money in the long run. Second, it is a way to behave responsibly toward the planet in which we all live. Third, customers notice. The word gets around. People like to spend their money with a company that respects the earth and treats its workers well. Reusing and recycling will do nothing but get more important as the world seems to get smaller, and Toyota is already a leader in that arena.

Concentrate on Flow

Flow, in Toyota's way of thinking, is the only means to achieve "lean" manufacturing.

Consider first how the huge majority of manufacturing companies around the world do their work. They are not lean. They in fact are "puffy," if I may use such a frivolous term to describe a serious problem. Manufacturers tend to think in terms not of flow but of economies of scale. This viewpoint results in areas around a typical plant that are used for items in bulk storage until there is need for them. On a grand scale, this tends to work, that is, if the economy is strong enough to push these items onto the line and through the plant.

I recently was given a tour through a facility that imprints logos and various designs on fabric such as T-shirts, button shirts, towels, and vests. Workers were stationed at various points on the line and were doing a fine job of adding color designs to the fabrics as they passed by. But there were dozens of areas around the plant that were indeed puffy—filled almost to the roof with shrink-wrapped goods awaiting processing. I asked my guide how long some of these materials might wait for processing, and she said up to three months. That is the very antithesis of the Toyota philosophy.

Ever since the Industrial Revolution, in the late seventeenth century, manufacturers have based their profits on producing things in such gargantuan quantities that the cost of an individual item is close to zero. After all, it was mass production that put millions of people to work and made it possible for most of them to afford washing machines and cell phones. Mass production was the key to profitability, and for many people it worked. But mass production assumes growing demand and a steady economy. When demand falters even slightly, the goods pile up. Or puff up, if you prefer.

For example, if you have a pencil handy, you might pick it up and examine it. Can you think of how much it would cost a company to produce just that one pencil for you? How much to design it, find the raw materials, such as graphite, rubber, and wood, mold it into the desired shape, and bore it on a lathe? (The town of Keswick, England, has a pencil museum for true aficionados. The graphite deposit near there contains the purest form of graphite for use in pencils and other markers.) To make just a single common #2 pencil, using the cheaper modern graphite powder, I'd guess about $380. Let's break it down:

Designer: 1 hour	$75
Wood cutter: 30 minutes	$32
Graphite miner: 20 minutes	$18
Rubber gatherer: 3 hours	$54
Lathe operator: 1.5 hours	$38
Gluer and sander: 7 minutes	$4.67
Sales representative: 10 minutes	$13
Supervisor: 5 hours	$145
Total:	$379.67

(The total does not include union dues, insurance benefits, or lunch breaks.)

That's the bad news for one pencil—you can't afford it. Now let's mass-produce that pencil. We'll gather all the raw materials from around the world as cheaply as possible. We'll work from one design with one color and use professional machine operators and pay them the going rate. And let's say we want to produce 100 million pencils. So now how much will that one pencil cost you? At that scale, there's no coin small enough to make the transaction. Give me a dime and I'll give you a dozen pencils. (Everyone says that pencils are a dime a dozen.)

The same pencil that once cost us 380 bucks is now a giveaway item. If you drop it on the floor, it's not even worth picking up.

How can that be? The answer is mass production and the economies of scale.

No one is arguing that mass production doesn't work. But, in the same vein, no one denies that mass-production profitability depends on a variety of uncontrollable factors. (Some people also argue that just-in-time doesn't work in emergency situations, such as when one needs to get medicines to an earthquake site or ramp up for an unforeseen war. They may be right. On the other hand, virtually no system is guaranteed to provide for emergencies—not even stockpiling.)

Here's a good rule of thumb: If flexibility and customer choice are not important, then mass-produce and enjoy the profits that come from massive scale. This is exactly what Henry Ford did with his early vehicles, and the profits came pouring in. He had not the slightest interest in asking customers what they wanted. He cared only about telling customers what they could have and at what price they could have it, consistent with his profitability. On the other hand, if you are giving customers *total* say over the vehicles they purchase, then mass production is exactly the wrong way to go. Lean production is your only option. In mass production, you dare not stop the line or profits will vanish. In lean production, you must stop the line in order to prevent defects from flowing downstream.

One mistake that many manufacturing companies make is to look at Ford-style mass production from the 1920s and assume that it will work today. It won't. Even Ford acknowledges that. Customers are a long, long way down the road and are completely accustomed to getting products exactly the way they want them. If you order a Dell computer online, for example, you can demand custom configurations and follow the trail of *your* computer online as it is being put together. Dell doesn't necessarily want to make computers this way; customers simply give the company no choice.

Mass production theory gets us a pencil for free, or nearly so. But what if what we really want is a car? A good car? A good cheap car that won't break down or shimmy at speeds over 50 mph?

For that, we need flow.

Toyota considers flow to be exactly the right term, as in a flowing stream. The early contributors to the process are upstream; the later contributors of value are downstream. Lean production means the stream is flowing at just the right speed for us to get the work done and maintain high quality.

If stream and flow are good images for lean production, what are the images for mass production? Pond and stagnation.

Look at any pond or lake. Do you see rocks or boulders in the water? You might see a few, but common sense tells you that most of the rocks are under water, hidden from sight.

Now look at any stream or creek. What do you see in addition to the water flowing by? You can see all the rocks, pebbles, and boulders, because the stream flows by and through them without covering them up.

Now, if we extend the metaphor just a bit, we can call those rocks and boulders problems or defects in the production process. A pond (mass production) covers up all but a few of the rocks. Those are hidden defects that will not appear to workers until it's too late to fix them. As a metaphor, it accounts for Detroit's frequent recall of hundreds of thousands of vehicles owing to a defect that remained hidden until hapless owners started driving the cars. The rocks (defects) always show up—it's simply a question of when.

The flowing stream (lean production) reveals virtually all of the rocks (defects) to anyone who happens by; the problems can therefore be fixed without being pushed on down the line. If *kaizen* is the goal—and it should be—then proper flow rate is the only way to find and fix problems.

If you understand the metaphor, you can understand why the Toyota Production System works so well. Defects are never passed from upstream workers to downstream workers because the defects are apparent—thanks to the proper flow of the production line. It isn't too fast (like a flood that covers everything as well) and it isn't too slow (like a pond that can stagnate and hide defects for a long time).

Flow is the key. It is among the most important concepts that have enabled Toyota to rule the automotive world.

An Answer to the Quality Riddle

Why is Toyota completely lean, whereas 98 percent of other companies that try to copy TPS are only somewhat lean?

The answer is complex. But if you've read this far, chances are you can think of three or four reasons. It's a good exercise. Try to come up with a few before reading my response. By the way, there is no definitive right answer.

_____

_____

_____

_____

Here's what I think:

Starting from zero is generally easier and more efficient than retrofitting.

It's true that Sakichi Toyoda and Kiichiro Toyoda created most of the principles that are now commonplace in industry, such as just-in-time and "go to the source" for answers while getting your hands dirty.

That may have been enough to ensure that Toyota would become a world-class automotive company. The truth is, we will never know. World War II was a seminal event in world history. Some countries were triumphant, and some were devastated. Japan was devastated. The Toyoda founders swept away the ashes and saw that there was nothing left to build with—there were not even any customers except for the occupation army. Toyota could lock up and go home, or it could start over. It started over. In building the new Toyota from the ground up, the leaders started with lessons learned and created a new do-or-die culture that would either succeed beyond anyone's dreams or fail miserably. There was no middle ground.

While it's impossible to think of building from devastation as an advantage, it was at least...different. Detroit's carmakers, after the war, went back to the same old production line. They, too, had no choice. People wanted cars now, and Detroit delivered. As Toyota started to rock the world with its bold new production ideas, Detroit tried to retrofit, but it was stuck with antiquated systems.

Toyota started lean and stayed there. It had no old culture to deal with, no old ways of doing things, no poorly designed production lines to work around or workers who needed to be cleansed of old ideas before they could accept new ones. For example, GM reports a 25 percent absentee rate routinely year after year. The Toyota plant in Kentucky reports a 2 percent absentee rate. The workers are from the same American culture, but, in agreeing to work in the Toyota culture, they are forced to accept the new reality that attendance is mandatory. One American supervisor at the plant, speaking half in jest, said that employees there are expected to do only two things: show up for work and pull the cord if there's a problem.

Ask building contractors which is easier: starting from scratch or retrofitting into old construction. The answer will give you a big clue as to why Toyota is the only truly lean production company in the world.

For a larger and more dramatic example, look at the United States. For more than two centuries, the United States has been the single most successful country in the world by almost any measure: more scientific patents than any other country in the world, more movies, more amusement parks, more manufacturing plants, more personal income, more highways, more libraries, more movement of workers from lower class to middle class, more worldwide corporations, more newspapers, more air conditioners, ubiquitous electric power, and on and on.

Why is that? The answer is as complex as the subject, of course, but here's one explanation that might work for you: America started from scratch, centuries after all the other now-industrialized nations. Europe, in 1776, had been working on the philosophy of an ideal political structure for generations. Its brightest thinkers had been pondering and writing about the question for even longer. Monarchy worked once in a while, parliamentary divisions worked once in a while—lots of ideas worked occasionally. But what would work long term?

America's founders pondered this question publicly and came up with the basis for a republic—made up of an executive branch, a large congressional branch, and a judicial branch—that so far has stood the test of time. The founders may or may not have been smarter than the politicians we have today in all the major countries, but they had one advantage that no other country has today: They started from zero, after rejecting a monarchy.

There is wonderful liberty to be found in building an infrastructure— with all attendant philosophies—from the ground up. Toyota, to its everlasting credit, made profitable use of that freedom.

Understand That the Moment We Are Pleased with Ourselves Is the Moment We Start to Fail

Brother Lawrence, a medieval Franciscan monk, once wrote that he feared becoming too humble, lest he be proud of his humility.

Toyota, for all of its great advances, understands that it is a human enterprise subject to the variety of human failings. No organization can be perfect. Ask any Toyota executive, and he or she will tell you that staying focused on serving customers is the only antidote for human frailty. Once in a while, even Toyota forgets that, and the slide begins alarmingly quickly.

In early 2006, Toyota started losing ground as the world's most successful carmaker. Warnings showed up in print in automotive magazines. Dealers of other car brands whispered to customers that Toyota was no longer what it used to be. The alarms went off at the Toyota home office in Japan, as well. Executives went on the record saying that yes, the company had started to rest a bit on its famous laurels but that it had heard the wake-up call and was now more fully engaged in *kaizen* than ever. The slide stopped. By the end of the 2007 calendar year, Toyota stock was up where it should be, and its vehicles were once again looked upon favorably by customers.

The remarkable thing is not that Toyota allowed quality to slip slightly but that it immediately went public with the truth and promised to rectify the situation. That is a lesson most other carmakers fail to heed.

Anyone can see the power of such an honest way of looking at reality in Toyota's bottom-line figures for 2006.

Chapter Six

Financial Results and Leadership

In 2006, Toyota sold nearly 8 million vehicles under four brands: Toyota, Lexus, Daihatsu, and Hino. This makes Toyota the highest-selling automobile company on earth. In the same year, Toyota produced vehicles in 26 countries and had 280,000 employees.

Details for 2006

Net Revenues: $179,083,000,000
Operating Income: $15,990,000,000
Net Income: $11,681,000,000
Return on Equity: 14%
Net Income per share: $3.59
Total Assets: $244,587,000,000

The company steadily set new records in 2006. Compared to results for 2005:

- Revenue was up more than 13 percent
- Operating income was up more than 12 percent
- Vehicle production hit 7.71 million units, up 6.6 percent
- Of those 7.71 million, 4.68 million were produced in Japan, and 1.2 million were produced in North America
- Vehicle sales hit 7.97 million units, up 7.6 percent, with Japan and North America accounting for more than 60 percent of those sales
- Net income was up 17 percent

Katsuaki Watanabe, president, put this into perspective in an interview:

In 2006 we were able to increase vehicle sales...by actively rolling out new models in markets worldwide. In addition, sales of hybrid vehicles were brisk....To date, we have sold more than 600,000 hybrid vehicles....I believe that each vehicle we sell testifies to the trust customers place in us and represents an endorsement of the painstaking approach we take to manufacturing that we have upheld over the years.

President Watanabe, while not saying so, was a prime mover in this stellar success story. He embodies Toyota's reputation for hardheaded attention to details. Like a soldier who rises through the ranks from private to general, he came up through Toyota's internal departments, such as purchasing, planning, and administration. He made the board of directors—an extreme honor for anyone, let alone a hard-working foot soldier—in 1992. His professional emphasis has always been on finding and cutting out waste. That helps explain his dramatic global initiative aimed at cutting costs around the world.

Known as the Construction of Cost Competitiveness for the Twenty-First Century, or CCC-21, the program focused on making sure Toyota retains its leadership position in the face of new alliances from competitors. Nissan partnered with Renault to enjoy greater purchasing and benchmarking power. DaimlerChrysler, around the same time, was launched specifically to improve its position against Toyota. The world was grabbing hold of Toyota's coattails, and Mr. Watanabe understood that meant even greater reliance on *kaizen* for his company.

In its first five years of existence, Watanabe's CCC-21 found and eliminated $10 billion of wasted costs, principally through its newfound emphasis on bringing the *kaizen* way of life to suppliers. To many industry commentators, the really amazing thing was that he was able to enhance quality even while cutting costs, like a dieter who loses weight and gets stronger at the same time.

CCC-21 is an important reason why Toyota recorded the figures charted above—a net profit of around $17 billion, give or take a few million. And market capitalization passed $200 billion—at a time when its competitors were fighting just to stay even. It was a fight most of them lost.

Not content to rest even on these achievements, the president has notified the world that Toyota is now embarked on phase two of its waste-reduction program, called Value Innovation. Sakichi Toyoda, in looking to improve loom technology, went back to the very foundation of what makes a loom a loom. Similarly, his successors are going back to the heart of design and development of an automobile itself. If Toyota can integrate more systems from the foundation of a vehicle, it can decrease production time by reducing the number of components and again provide customers with even more value for their money.

From the start, Toyota has been perfectly clear about its mission, and that clarity continues to be cherished by its current president. As Watanabe said in a recent speech, "the world-class quality we have built is our lifeline."

Let's take a closer look at the executive team in place as of this writing, starting with Mr. Watanabe:

KATSUAKI WATANABE

When Katsuaki Watanabe took over the reins of Toyota Motor Corporation, in June 2005, he was not the most obvious choice. Traditionally, the top executive comes from manufacturing or sales or marketing. Mr. Watanabe, however, came from the cost-cutting department. Choosing him was emblematic of Toyota's bold new emphasis on making money and providing customers with more value by cutting costs.

Although an employee of the company for 40 years, Watanabe's primary experience was not with cars but on the periphery, where he made his presence felt. His first job, for example, was managing the company cafeteria. He was famous for keeping a data-filled journal that enabled him to track waste in its many forms. Recalling those days, he said, "People thought it was strange that a guy was taking data in the kitchen. There was so much waste, so I saw there was clearly room for improvement."

With his own interests in eliminating waste dovetailing so well with the company's, he rose quickly through the ranks. He was named to the board of directors in 1992. Thanks in part to his leadership, the company went on an aggressive cost-cutting program that enabled it to increase quality while eliminating literally billions of dollars in overhead and waste costs.

Perhaps most tellingly, he was called "Mister *Kaizen*" within the organization—high praise indeed.

International journals noticed the improvements. Under Watanabe's leadership, according to *Business Week* in 2005, "one team disassembled the horns made by a Japanese supplier and found ways to eliminate six of twenty-eight components, resulting in a 40% cost reduction." That's just one example.

While other carmakers were reporting shrinking profits in 2006, Toyota marked about $17 billion in profits—its highest ever.

Here's what *Time* magazine said about Watanabe in a 2005 article:

> Katsuaki Watanabe, who takes over as CEO of Toyota in June, faces a huge task. There's no smoldering scandal to extinguish, no battered confidence to restore, no eroding margins to reverse. But that's the problem: Toyota's performance has been so consistently outstanding over the past decade that it's hard to see how Watanabe, 62, can lift the world's most profitable and valuable automaker— and perhaps the world's best company—to new heights.

The article goes on to praise Toyota's production system and the introduction of the Prius, two inescapable advantages that contribute to Toyota's bid for world dominance in making automobiles. Getting back to

Watanabe's personal style, it praises him for distinguishing himself "not by snipping ribbons on new plants or giving speeches, but as a behind-the-scenes cost cutter and logistical mastermind. Those are the skills Toyota needs if it is to expand its operations when other automakers are cutting back."

HIROSHI OKUDA

Rolling Stone magazine featured Okuda in its November 3, 2005, issue, saying that as chairman of Toyota, he

> envisioned the need for a hybrid car long before history demanded it. In the 1990s, at a time when oil prices were hitting rock bottom and America's SUV market was exploding, Okuda green lighted the engine technology that would usher in an era of fuel-efficient—and eventually zero-emission—cars. Today there are more than 350,000 Priuses on the road worldwide, and other automakers are racing to catch up with the 350 patents Toyota holds on gas-electric hybrids.

The article goes on to quote Okuda himself who, typically, has worked at Toyota for 50 years. "People and countries simply will no longer allow autos to damage their living environments or the Earth's ecosystems." Okuda chose the name Prius because it means *to go before* in Latin. The Prius has certainly gone before all other hybrids, outpacing them in quality and sales before the rest of the automotive world has had a chance to even think about making a good-quality hybrid at reasonable cost.

Toyota's own Web site describes him this way:

> Born in 1933—about the same time as Toyota itself—Hiroshi Okuda has been a member of the Board of Toyota Motor Corporation since 1982, and has been the Chairman of the Board since 1999. Mr. Okuda was the president of Toyota from 1995 to 1999, and is also a director of KDDI Corporation. Hiroshi Okuda joined Toyota in 1955, at about the time of the company's entrance to the United States market. He mainly worked in Toyota's international operations, and oversaw preparation of manufacturing plants in North America.

Perhaps not surprisingly, Okuda holds a black belt in judo.

FUJIO CHO

Board member Cho thinks long term and worldwide. Born in 1937, he is a streamliner. He graduated from the University of Tokyo in 1960 and became a production specialist. He is a third *dan in kendo.*

Here's what *Business Week* said about him in a 2003 article:

Fujio Cho has a soft spot for Kentucky bluegrass. Before becoming president of Toyota Motor Corp. in 1999, he earned his spurs as a global manager during a seven-year stint overseeing the company's main U.S. manufacturing base in Kentucky. One day not long after his arrival, a rare snowstorm swept in, threatening to seize up Toyota's famed just-in-time production. But when Cho set foot in the Georgetown factory that morning, fearing the worst, he found it humming. "Workers either spent the night at the plant or set out to work three or four hours early to make sure the line would start on time," he recalls. "It's something I'll never forget."

Mr. Cho manages to keep control of a spectrum of challenges he faces, particularly overseas—even in Japan. With his help, Toyota has managed to maintain its 42 percent share of the Japanese market. Europe, traditionally hard ground for Toyota, is now a source of profit. Toyota's Yaris, a subcompact made in Valenciennes, France, is a hit with European drivers. Toyota totaled up a $30 million operating profit in Europe in 2006.

Toyota is now expanding all over the world: increased production in France and Great Britain, a new $800 million pickup truck plant in Texas, and another plant in Tianjin, China, to make luxury Crowns. Mr. Cho expects the company to sell 400,000 cars a year to the Chinese and to bring Toyota's share of the global vehicle market up to 15 percent.

AKIO TOYODA, SON OF SHOICHIRO TOYODA

Akio, born in 1957, helped to get Toyota out of a Chinese joint venture that failed to produce results. He has started a Web-based retailing venture in Japan and is currently executive vice president in charge of purchasing, quality, product management, IT, and transport. While time will tell if he has the timber required to lead Toyota, he no doubt has unmatched "institutional memory" that will not only aid in his career but keep Toyota's long-standing principles at the fore in any undertaking.

Clearly, Toyota places a premium on high-caliber executives with vision and an enduring sense of what it means to be a Toyota man or woman.

Chapter Seven

Toyota Invents the Future...Again

LEXUS: LUXURY JAPANESE-STYLE

It was the biggest and most carefully kept secret in the history of manufacturing: Toyota was thinking about building a luxury car.

This was a new dimension of bold thinking, especially for a company that had always been described as careful and deliberate. Let other carmakers produce an Edsel or a hard-top convertible and watch as they are laughed out of showrooms. Let the others waste years of development on concept cars that make the magazine covers but not the production line. Toyota made the small, high-performance, defect-free cars that their loyal customers around the world demanded, and that was the end of the story. Once in a while the market would shift toward giant gas-guzzlers or sexy Mustangs; Toyota would always keep working at what it did best. Year after year, decade after decade, the Corollas and Camrys and Cressidas kept rolling off the line, and people bought them at a steady pace.

There was another consideration. In the late 1970s and early 1980s, the two words one never saw together were "Japanese" and "luxury." For a thousand years, Japan eschewed any hint of softness. Luxury was a sign of weakness. Showing off was unthinkable. Japanese drivers tended to prefer cars with neutral colors because they didn't show dirt the way dark colors do, and they didn't stand out in traffic. A company president and a cafeteria cook sat side by side on the bullet train into the city, just two salaried workers with different jobs. A Japanese adage suggests that the nail that sticks out gets the hammer.

Prospects for a Japanese elite car were as soft as the leather seats in the high-end Cadillacs. Let the Germans and the Italians and even the staid British make luxury motor cars. Rolls Royce, Mercedes, BMW, Jaguar, and Maserati were already household brands—if your household was a mansion. Those brands were so well entrenched in the minds of the entire car-buying public that going up against them was like throwing snowballs at battleships.

There was one other thing against the idea: the image that luxury customers had of themselves. Would the president of Ogilvy and Mather advertising agency in New York ever envision himself meeting clients for a round of golf in a, well, a, uh, that is, umm, a *Japanese* luxury car? Even if he liked the car, he could hear his buddies saying, "What's the matter, Bill? The Rolls in the shop again? Say, what kind of car is that, anyway?"

The man who would become chief engineer on Toyota's luxury concept car, Ichiro Suzuki, knew all this and much more. All the signs were against it. Toyota stood for quality and low price, not luxury. It was the common-sense brand, like Ivory soap and Maytag washing machines and John Deere tractors. If you don't want to spend a whole lot and if you want a car that won't spend days in the repair shop, buy a Toyota. If you want luxury, buy a Rolls.

Further, the chief engineer understood that the luxury brands started out as luxury brands. There was never a cheap Rolls-Royce. A Jaguar didn't come in a knock-down version. Mercedes didn't make a compact, low-price model.

A Puzzler?

Can you think of a brand that started out as a low-end or middle-of-the-road product and is now the high-priced or luxury item in its category?

_____

_____

If you're having a hard time, so am I.

Subaru started out as a moderately priced family car. Its highly regarded four-wheel-drive technology pushed it ahead of the pack and allowed it to offer higher-priced sedans, wagons, and SUVs. But it is rare for technology to pull a brand up in price.

This may be one of the primary reasons that you won't see the Toyota brand anywhere on a Lexus. Branding theory argues that however a company positions its brand when it first comes out—that's where it stays.

Stacked up, all of those considerations seemed insurmountable. It simply didn't make sense for Toyota even to think about a luxury car for the world's elite buyers. There was only one factor on the side of going for it: Toyota is in the innovation business. An important corollary to that truth is the fact that Toyota's investment in its people is wholehearted. Odds were far and away against success, and everyone at Toyota knew that. What Toyota executives also knew was that if anyone could go up against the big guys and win, it would be people who drew a Toyota paycheck—a comparatively small paycheck, at that. No company has more employees who are driven to perfection than Toyota. The skill and the do-or-die attitude of its engineers provided the springboard for Toyota's leap into the elite motor car business. For Toyota, a company used to risk, this was taking a big-league chance at tarnishing the name forever.

"Even if the target seems so high as to be unachievable at first glance," Ichiro Suzuki said in an interview, "if you explain the necessity to all the people involved and insist upon it, everyone will become enthusiastic in the spirit of challenge, will work together, and achieve it."

There was plenty of challenge to go around, and so the company started in the typical Toyota way. It designated the luxury-car project "F1" for Flagship, as an indication that this was the start of a new day at Toyota. It flew the project team of 20 engineers to those areas of the world where luxury buyers roamed free in their natural habitats. The team drew chalk circles, and stood in them, and observed. What they discovered was stunning.

Where better to start than in Beverly Hills?

Los Angeles is car central. In L.A. you are what you eat and you are what you drive. Nobody walks in L.A. Everybody rides. People regard their cars as extensions of themselves. If you are wealthy in L.A., you have two ways to go. You can go retro with an antique Rolls or Bentley. Or you can go top-of-the-line with anything from a Maserati to a supercharged Lotus Exige. One thing you do for sure is go to the toniest restaurants—the ones with unlisted phone numbers.

So the F1 project team went to those restaurants, as well. They didn't go for the food. They went for the cars. At the trendy clubs and restaurants, one class of people determines a patron's status: the valet parking guys. Gossip columnists for the *Hollywood Reporter* ask these guys who's in and who's out. If you're in, you drive the kind of car that they park in front of the building so that everyone else can see what the standard is. If you're out, your car goes to a lot somewhere in Pasadena and you get it back an hour after you want it. The team watched open-mouthed as the little red British sports cars and custom rod jobs and glossy Rolls-Royces got the prime slots. Mercedes and BMW didn't usually make the cut. The team realized that Americans were different from everyone else on earth—they allow valets to determine status!—and that this project was going to be tougher than anyone thought.

Several truths became quickly apparent. First, American luxury car buyers weren't trying to impress people with their money. They wanted to impress others with the level of service that they received and in fact felt they were entitled to. In Europe, noble birth got you a good table at the best places whether you had money or not. In America, you needed the right house and the right car and the right celebrity status to be similarly received.

Second, there was no consistency among luxury car buyers. Their only common criterion for buying a car seemed to be cost—until the team encountered old-money Eastern elites from the Main Line and Beacon Hill, who drove beat-up Chevys and didn't care what anybody thought. How on earth were they supposed to produce one car that this vast array of humanity would desire?

And, third, the team realized that none of these people had ever had any kind of experience with a Japanese car. Toyota's hard-earned reputation for value and minimal defects and highly engineered quality meant nothing to them because they had never heard of Toyota! The team members fought their feeling of foreboding by doing what they did best—research.

In city after city, from Houston to New York, Miami to San Francisco, they sat unseen behind one-way mirrors as affluent customers sat around conference-room tables with a moderator and discussed what they liked and didn't like about their cars. They listened to wealthy dowagers from Nob Hill and music producers in their mid-thirties from Greenwich Village and oil barons from Fort Worth. The groups seemed to divide naturally into two segments: domestic and import.

Those in the Cadillac crowd liked their comforts—the surround sound, the sink-into leather seats, the powerful thrum of the eight-cylinder engine, and the whirr of the electric windows—and they liked buying American-made cars. They had grown up with Lincolns and Caddies, and by heaven they were going to stay with them because Daddy would not have had it any other way.

The other group, the Mercedes and BMW people, cared nothing for American cars. (There's an old joke: Heaven is where the British make the laws, the Americans make up the military, the French make the meals, and the Germans make the cars. Hell is where the British make the meals, the French make the cars, the Americans make the laws, and the Germans make up the military.) These people truly believed that only Germans can make good cars. What they loved about the German cars was the engineering; they could live with the Germanic disdain for creature comforts.

The best bit of good news for the project team was the insight that luxury-car buyers of every stripe hated to take their cars in for maintenance, because they knew the dealership would stick them with the outrageous bill. People who didn't even bother to ask the purchase price of the vehicle felt like victims of the back-of-the-showroom pirates. This was a clear opening for the F1, and the team members whispered delightedly among themselves. The purchase price is not a factor! The repair cost is! We can beat these guys!

The bad news came afterward, relentlessly, in group after group: Not one of them would consider buying a Japanese luxury car. They didn't even know how to handle the question. It was like asking them if they would buy a yacht from Joe's Engine Repair shop. The most common response was: Japanese cars? Aren't they rather thin?

It Might Have Been Cheaper to Land a Corolla on the Moon

Toyota spent more money researching and developing the Lexus than has been spent on a comparable project by any other car company in history.

- More than $1 billion in research and development over six years
- 60 car designers
- 1,400 engineers
- 450 prototypes costing $250,000 each
- A satellite communications network between dealers and head-quarters
- A cost of up to $3 million to each of the 100 dealers in the United States just to join the franchise. Toyota maintained supervision of dealership quality.

Back in Japan, the research team sat with the senior executives and pondered where they stood. American luxury cars were too padded and cushy; European luxury cars were too stiff and balky, as if the engineers who designed the pistons also designed the seats. Toyota would have to find a middle ground.

Furthermore, a luxury car has to *look* like a luxury car. What's the point of driving a $40,000 F1 to Spago if some long-haired valet parks it in the spaces marked *Siberia?*

What was on everyone's mind but never spoken was the nagging suspicion that it would be a serious mistake to link the F1 with Toyota in any way.

Engineering concerns came first; appearance second. Luxury cars are judged by their ability to handle speeds in excess of 150 miles per hour. Americans, of course, are not allowed to drive that fast. Germans are. The company would test the car on German autobahns. The engine itself—an in-line, six-cylinder just like those of the European cars—seemed just the ticket. The chief engineer, however, thought differently, and he had the final say: a high-powered V8. There would be no second chances. A Japanese car more powerful than a BMW would get attention.

Suzuki wanted good fuel economy, as well. The engineers worked around the clock to eliminate unnecessary waste, finding most of it in the undercarriage. In tests, the F1 breezed in at 23 miles per gallon. In your face, Mercedes.

Now the name. With fear and trembling, a new team came back from the United States with difficult advice for Eiji Toyoda: not a Toyota. He listened to the arguments carefully and said he agreed. They pushed a bit further: and not in the regular distribution channels. People would not spend $40,000 on the F1 when it was sitting next to a $16,000 Cressida.

Eiji agreed to that, too, knowing that the expense of a new dealer network would be astronomical.

The team had hired New York consultants to provide some good names for the F1. "Alexis" came closest to the mark but was not quite right. Someone tried a variation of it: Lexus. And there it was.

The car designers worked for two years in clay, building half-scale and full-scale models, 450 of them, all by hand with intensive labor. They molded and gouged and worked until at last the shape emerged that simply had to be it. It was beautiful in an understated, Japanese way. The colors? Nine of them, all exquisite.

There would be two models, it was decided, the ES250 and the larger LS400. The ES250 would compete with Honda's new Acura model at the same price point. The LS400 would compete with no other car. It would be the best automobile in the world.

Dealers were a relatively simple matter. Twelve hundred people applied for the 100 dealerships, paying from $2 million to $3 million for the privilege of selling the finest car in the world. Toyota made it clear that the new dealer showrooms and garages would themselves be the best in the world.

The last skeptics who had to be convinced were the automobile journalists—a savvy cabal of writers and aficionados who could make or break any car brand on earth. In May 1989, Toyota flew them all to Germany for open-road tests against all comers. The Lexus won them over handily.

The last nail in the coffin of the Western competitors was a demonstration for the journalists. Toyota engineers put a LS400 on a lift so that the wheels were inches off the ground and started the engine. Then one of them filled a glass full with water and placed the glass on the hood of the car. The water was motionless. When another engineer got inside the driver's seat and raced the engine, the water was still as quiet as the surface of a pond. The writers dropped their notebooks and applauded for a long, long time.

There was one final test, the biggest of all. Would the American public buy a car that had "Japanese" and "luxury" in the same sentence? The cars went on sale September 1, 1989. The only problem was that customers shrugged at the base price and demanded the custom model at $43,000. It was a new era. In its first full year of sales, Lexus virtually matched Mercedes and BMW.

The advertising slogan for Lexus got it right as well: "the relentless pursuit of perfection."

PRIUS: NEW THINKING FOR A NEW AGE

If the Lexus changed how the world thinks about luxury cars, Prius changed how the world thinks about cars.

Toyota had pioneered lighter and leaner cars that sipped gas rather than gulped it. It had shaved two ounces from the steering wheel, reduced the number of pieces of connecting hardware like nuts and bolts to the bare minimum consistent with performance and safety, and combined and sliced off and eliminated everything possible from top to bottom, front to back. There was nothing left to cut.

Unless...it could alter the way the engine uses fuel for power.

In 1994, the company made the earth-shaking decision to change the nature of a car entirely—from fuel-based to a combination of fuel and battery power. In other words, it would create a hybrid, a new entity derived from two previously existing entities. When one thinks about it, who else but Toyota was likely to do this? No other company is so dedicated to constant innovation. No other car company sees it as part of its mission to make the world a better place. Of course Toyota would be the first to risk a fortune on this never-seen-before car. Honda had made a halfhearted stab at a hybrid a year before Toyota, but of course it was Toyota that would make it happen.

And like the Wright brothers at Kitty Hawk, the Prius almost didn't get off the ground. The prototype models, it seems, wouldn't start.

The G-21 team (shorthand for Global 21st Century) tweaked the software and reconfigured the electrical systems for weeks. Finally the car started. It rolled down the road cheerfully for several hundred yards until it stopped dead. This was not a good start for the world's first global car.

Two years earlier, Eiji Toyoda, the engineering genius who had guided Toyota from a government truck manufacturer after the war to a world-leading car company, had come to a remarkable point in his life. He doubted that the automobile as the world knew it had much of a future. This would be like the chairman of Heinz fretting that the new generation would no longer enjoy the taste of ketchup. In fact, Eiji Toyoda had reason to worry. Oil prices were moving inexorably upward, with no end in sight. The world's major players saw signs of growing crisis in the Middle East, home of the planet's largest oil reserves. Cars were getting bigger again. Drivers (especially Americans) were starting to demand more sport utility vehicles with their four-wheel drive capability and blithely ignored the fact that SUVs got fewer than 18 miles per gallon. Countries like China were joining the clamor for more vehicles and more gas from a dwindling number of suppliers. People seemed willing to pay any price for gas, but Eiji Toyoda knew there was a ceiling. When drivers hit that ceiling, whatever it was, the car culture would come crashing down.

When Eiji worries, everybody at Toyota worries. Yoshiro Kimbara, the man in charge of research and development, understood the concern and did something about it. He started G-21 with two goals: to get better fuel economy somehow and somehow to develop new ways to produce cars. His target was 47 miles per gallon, a breathtakingly high number for the time and half again better than the Corolla was getting.

The project needed a *serious* engineer to lead the way. It found one in Takeshi Uchiyamada, the noise and vibration expert who understood hard work and loved a challenge. His first request was to begin building a superior engine and transmission the old way but using the latest technology. It was the logical and conservative way to do it. His superiors came back forcefully: no. Build something new that doesn't yet exist. Build a hybrid.

This wasn't exactly new. Several Japanese car companies had been fiddling for years with the idea of marrying a gas engine to a battery-powered engine. Several designers thought they could get the batteries to recharge every time the car braked. But the time was not right. It would be too expensive, and gas was still affordable. Motivation to invest in the necessary research then was low. But the times had changed again, and the wind was blowing toward developing hybrid technology.

Uchiyamada resisted forcefully but respectfully, citing the long-term expense and drain on resources that even Toyota could ill afford. Still, the word filtered down the line indirectly, as it always does: Do it anyway. Build a concept hybrid powertrain for the 1995 show in Tokyo a year from now. Oh, and to keep our competitors at bay, would you be so good as to improve gas mileage 100 percent? In classic Japanese understatement, Uchiyamada, now a member of the board, said, "At that moment I felt they demanded too much." It would be like a defender of the Alamo saying that Colonel Travis, in asking them to forfeit their lives, had demanded too much. And, like the Colonel, the Toyota executives seemed to be saying, yes, it is demanding too much. Are there any other questions?

At any other car company, an order to double gas mileage in 12 months would have been taken as an absurdity; the hands-on people who were involved would have surely resigned. At Toyota, it was just another day at the factory.

Uchiyamada's team had lengthy experience in mechanics, but little experience with the high-tech electronic components and massively powered batteries that the G-21 (now called Prius) called for. From the wide range of potential directions to pursue in models and drive trains, the team quickly narrowed the list to the four that would offer the best fuel efficiency. In June 1995, it chose the one that had the best chance of working and put all its money into one power train design.

Prius Timeline

January 1992—Toyota announces its plans to develop and market vehicles with the lowest possible level of emissions.

September 1993—Toyota creates G-21, a committee to research cars for the twenty-first century. The "G" stands for "global" and the "21" for "twenty-first century."

January 1994—Takeshi Uchiyamada takes over as leader of the G-21 project team. Later, he heads up engineering for the Prius.

Late 1994—The G-21 team, with a mission to build a car that is environmentally friendly while ensuring that it is modern in all senses of the word, designs a concept car with a hybrid engine for the 1995 Tokyo Motor Show. The concept car is named "Prius."

October 1995—The Prius concept car is shown at the 31st Tokyo Motor Show. It steals the show.

July 1996—The model designed by Irwin Lui of Toyota's Calty Design Studio, in Newport Beach, Calif., is selected to go into production.

Late 1996—Prototype test driving begins.

October 1997—The Prius is officially unveiled to the press.

December 1997—The Prius goes on sale to the public in Japan, two years ahead of a hybrid by any other manufacturer.

August 2000—The Prius is launched in the United States as a 2001 model, with a manufacturer's suggested retail price of $19,995.

January 2001—Toyota reports 5,562 Prius sales in the United States for the period August–December 2000.

January 2002—Toyota reports U.S. Prius sales of 15,556 in 2001, up 180% from 2000.

January 2003—Toyota reports sales of 20,119 Prius hybrids in the United States during 2002.

April 2003—Toyota introduces the second-generation 2004 Prius at the New York Auto Show. Its price remains unchanged.

July 2006—Total Prius sales top 500,000.

Toyota executives in California had heard of the G-21, of course, but doubted that Americans would consider such a creation to be a car at all. Nevertheless, Californians, laboring for decades under a cloud of smog that seemed like a permanent fixture over Los Angles, were demanding greater emission controls for vehicles. Even the future seemed to be confused about what it wanted to do.

Back in Japan, the confusion centered on batteries. Sometimes in hot weather the batteries caught fire. In cold weather, below 14 degrees F, they shut down entirely. To the engineers, these were merely problems that needed some tender, loving *kaizen*. After nearly a year of microscopic fussing, the team squeezed out the improvement the bosses had demanded: 66 miles per gallon.

In Japan, Prius was a hit. In its first full year, it sold over 18,000 units. In the States, the story was different. Some execs wanted Prius in an SUV that would carry the batteries more readily; some thought that an SUV was the wrong message for a "global" car whose mission was to reduce consumption of fossil fuels. Customers in test drives didn't much care for it either and wrote down a litany of complaints. The brakes felt funny. The interior was "too Japanese" for American tastes. The trunk was too small.

Even worse, the typical buyer for whom the car was created—the "green" folks who still wore 1960s-style ponytails and built compost bins in the back yard—didn't much care for it. The air went out of the hybrid balloon.

These were setbacks, clearly, but the world *would* have a hybrid. It was simply a matter of time. Toyota decided to press forward. The two biggest puzzles were how many cars to make and how much to charge for them.

Headquarters wanted a Camry-level price tag over $20,000. The Americans had seen consumer resistance and lobbied for much less. Everyone from makers to dealers took a cut and launched the Prius for five bucks under $20,000. Toyota lost money on each car sold.

An article in *Car and Driver* magazine didn't help: "The Prius alternatively lurches and bucks down the road, its engine noise swelling and subsiding for no apparent reason."

What few of the experts counted on was the self-image of Prius owners. Prius made a statement—the exact statement that the members of a small but powerful segment of potential buyers wanted to make about themselves. "I care about burning less fuel. I care about greatly improved emissions. I care so much that I *don't* care about how the car looks or about its tendency to lurch. I'm driving a Prius because I want you to care too."

What clinched the deal for Prius sales was the movie star Leonardo DiCaprio driving one off the Hollywood lot in 2001. Cameron Diaz bought one soon after. At the 2003 Academy Awards, Calista Flockhart and Harrison Ford proudly disembarked from a chauffeur-driven Prius, to the delight of photographers. What's good enough for Indiana Jones is good enough for the rest of us. Sales took off.

Second-generation cars turned even more heads. Faster, with more power, they used even less fuel and reduced emissions closer to zero. Sales in America doubled, to nearly 54,000 cars in 2004, and price seemed no object to people who waited months in line to get one. One of the senior U.S. executives enthused to reporters: "It's the hottest car we've ever had."

The others were sure to follow. GM, whose vice chairman sniffed at the Prius in 2004 as an "interesting curiosity," is now the proud producer of a full line of hybrid pickups and SUVs. What changed, beside the overt success of Prius? In 2004, gasoline was $1.49 a gallon. Now that gasoline costs have failed to find a ceiling, everyone is a believer. Mercedes-Benz (Mercedes-Benz!) showcases its diesel-electric sedans. Look for a quarter of a million hybrid Fords by 2009. Nissan, ever in the shadow of Toyota, is now enthusiastic about hybrids.

In 2006, *Fortune* magazine put it all into perspective. "If Toyota can continue to reduce costs, and it most probably will, the potential for hybrids may be nearly unlimited. With its huge head start, better technology, enormous scale, and powerful will to make hybrids an everyday alternative to the internal combustion engine—a combination no other auto maker can match—it's hard to see Toyota not dominating the industry for years to come."

What's not hard to see is Kiichiro Toyoda, holding the company together by sheer force of will after the ashes of World War II had been cleared away. How often had he been tempted to lock the doors and go home to his gardens? How often had he wondered whether the divine wind that had protected his beloved country for so long had at last retreated to the far side of Mount Fuji, never to return again?

It doesn't take much imagination to see him pulling over that chair to a corner of the first factory and standing on it, the sign in his hand. We can see him tacking up that legendary sign and stepping down from the chair, then backing away to admire his work. What we can never know is whether he had even a fleeting glimpse of the future as he thought about those world-changing words: Just in Time.

Bibliography

BOOKS

Ellis, Joseph. *American Creation: Triumphs and Tragedies at the Founding of the Republic.* New York: Knopf, 2007.

Farnie, D. A., Takeshi Abe, David Jeremy, Tetsuro Nakaoka, and John F. Wilson, eds. *Region and Strategy in Britain and Japan: Business in Lancashire and Kansai, 1890–1990.* New York: Routledge, 2000.

Ford, Henry. *Today and Tomorrow,* reprint edition. Portland, OR: Productivity Press, 1988.

Imai, Masaaki. *Kaizen: The Key to Japan's Competitive Success.* New York: McGraw-Hill, 1986.

Lacey, Robert. *Ford: The Men and the Machine.* Boston: Little, Brown and Co., 1986.

Liker, Jeffrey K. *The Toyota Way: 14 Management Principles from the World's Greatest Manufacturer.* New York: McGraw-Hill, 2004.

Magee, David. *How Toyota Became Number One.* New York: Penguin Books Ltd., 2007.

Smiles, Samuel. *Self-Help.* The Echo Library, 2006.

Togo, Yukiyasu and William Wartman. *Against All Odds: The Story of the Toyota Motor Corporation and the Family That Created It.* New York: St. Martin's Press, 1993.

Toyoda, Eiji. *Fifty Years in Motion.* New York: Kodansha America, 1987.

Womack, James P., Daniel T. Jones, and Daniel Roos. *The Machine That Changed the World: The Story of Lean Production.* New York: Harper Perennial, 1991.

WEB SITES

www.loc.gov. The Library of Congress is the largest library in the world. It makes its resources available to Congress and to the American people.

www.lexus.com. This is the official Web site for all things Lexus.

www.time.com. This site is managed by Time, Inc., personnel and provides topic searches free of charge.

www.toyota.com. This is the main Web site offered by Toyota. It provides some history and a thorough look at Toyota manufacturing facilities around the world.

www.toyota.co.jp/Museum. Toyota in Japan maintains the Toyota Automobile Museum and this Web site.

ARTICLES

Dawson, Chester. "Blazing the Toyota Way." *Business Week* (May 24, 2004): 22.

Editorial. "Lean Machines." *The Economist* (September 22, 1990): 16–17.

Kageyama, Yuri. "Toyota Beats GM in Global Production." Associated Press, (January 28, 2008).

Krisher, Tom. "Toyota Takes 1Q Sales Lead from General Motors." Associated Press, (April 23, 2008).

Reingold, Edward. "Time 100: Eiji Toyoda." *Time Asia* (August 23, 1999): 4–6.

Staff. "The Road Warrior: Hiroshi Okuda." *Rolling Stone* (November 3, 2005): 18–19.

Taylor, Alex III. "The Birth of the Prius." *Fortune* (March 6, 2006): 111–24.

Wada, Kazuo. "The Fable of the Birth of the Japanese Automobile Industry: A Reconsideration of the Toyoda—Platt Agreement of 1929." *Business History* 48, no. 1 (January 2006): 90–118.

Womack, Jim. "Just Plain Wrong." *IEEE Manufacturing Engineer* (February–March 2006): 18.

Index

About the Author

K. DENNIS CHAMBERS is Founder of Chambers Communications, specializing in advertising and marketing communications, technical writing, and business writing. He is an adjunct professor of English at NECC and corporate trainer with several national companies. He is the author of *Writing to Get Action* and *The Entrepreneur's Guide to Writing Business Plans and Proposals* (Praeger 2007).